SIMPLE
SPICE
VEGETARIAN

SIMPLE
SPICE
VEGETARIAN

BY CYRUS TODIWALA

EASY INDIAN
VEGETARIAN RECIPES
FROM JUST 10 SPICES

MITCHELL BEAZLEY

An Hachette UK Company
www.hachette.co.uk

First published in Great Britain in 2020 by
Mitchell Beazley, an imprint of
Octopus Publishing Group Ltd
Carmelite House
50 Victoria Embankment
London EC4Y 0DZ
www.octopusbooks.co.uk
www.octopusbooksusa.com

Text copyright © Cyrus Todiwala 2020

Distributed in the US by
Hachette Book Group
1290 Avenue of the Americas
4th and 5th Floors
New York, NY 10104

Distributed in Canada by
Canadian Manda Group
664 Annette St.
Toronto, Ontario, Canada M6S 2C8

ISBN 978-1-78472-576-1

A CIP catalogue record for this book is
available from the British Library.

Printed and bound in China

10 9 8 7 6 5 4 3 2 1

Publisher's note:
Standard level spoon measurements
are used in all recipes.
1 tablespoon = one 15ml spoon
1 teaspoon = one 5ml spoon

Fan assisted oven temperatures are given.

Both imperial and metric measurements
have been given in all recipes. Use one set
of measurements only and not a mixture
of both.

Eggs are medium unless otherwise stated.

All cheeses used should be vegetarian and
should not contain animal rennet.

Publisher: Denise Bates
Art Director: Yasia Williams-Leedham
Designer: www.gradedesign.com
Senior Editor: Louise McKeever
Photographer: Matt Russell
Food stylist: Sunil Vijayakar and
Flossy McAslan
Prop stylist: Alexander Breeze
Copy Editor: Kay Delves
Production Controller: Emily Noto

CONTENTS

Introduction

First of all, thank you for buying my book.

A number of factors inspired me to create this vegetarian and vegan collection of my recipes. The current growth of interest in vegetarian food and the changes many of us are making to our eating habits have sparked a wonderful new wave of creative vegetarian cooking. As far as Indian food is concerned, of course, that is nothing new. Over a third of the population of India are vegetarian and, as a country, it has the largest vegetarian population in the world. The traditions and range of Indian vegetarian food are so rich, varied and inventive that a hundred cookbooks would not be enough to do it justice and I could spend decades exploring the diversity and breadth of the vegetarian recipes of the Indian subcontinent. In my restaurant Café Spice Namasté we have adapted many of these to use seasonal British vegetables very successfully.

I do not count myself as a strict vegetarian but I can happily go for days without meat or fish if what I get to eat is delicious and creative. I do have to draw the line at eggs, however. As a Parsee, life without eggs is not worth living and I would struggle on a vegan diet for that reason. We Parsees love the egg so much I could have given you a hundred Parsee-inspired egg recipes. I restrained myself, however, and the egg chapter contains recipes from all over India.

Another area of restraint crucial to the concept of this book is in my use of spices. I am very aware of the reputation Indian food can have, and the fear of some cooks that they are going to need a cupboard bursting with hundreds of different spices to cook it successfully. I use only ten spices throughout this book. So if you make sure you have those ten to hand, the recipes will be simple to make. Of course, I'm always tempted as a chef to use more, and had to make some hard decisions about what to leave out. My choice was driven by considerations including how widely a spice can be used – its versatility – and how easy it is to get hold of. You can see my choice of ten really versatile and readily available spices on page 8.

I've divided the book into chapters that are loosely based on different types of meal. This can only be a rough guide, especially when it comes to Mains and Easy Lunches & Snacks. One person's snack might be a main meal for another person, and vice versa, of course. I would also encourage you to mix and match dishes and try serving combinations. A lot of these recipes lend themselves very well to being served together.

You might think some of the recipes and their ingredients lists look long. Please don't be put off, however. In many it is just a question of grabbing ingredients out of your cupboard or fridge. I also like to explain how to do things rather than assume knowledge, so sometimes longer recipes mean I'm just being helpful and giving some tips and alternatives along the way. The main thing is to enjoy experimenting and make these recipes your own. Have fun.

Cyrus Todiwala

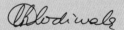

The 10 Spice Box ingredients (pages 10–11):

1 **Red chilli** (dried, crushed & powder)
2 **Fennel seeds**
3 **Cinnamon** (sticks & ground)
4 **Saffron** (threads)
5 **Cumin** (seeds & ground)
6 **Cardamom** (pods & ground)
7 **Ground turmeric**
8 **Coriander** (seeds & ground)
9 **Nutmeg** (whole & ground or grated)
10 **Black mustard seeds**

Other useful ingredients:

1 **Fresh herbs** (coriander, mint, basil & parsley)
2 **Curry leaves**
3 **Garlic**
4 **Fresh ginger**
5 **Onions** (all types)
6 **Fresh chillies** (red & green)
7 **Limes & lemons**
8 **Dried herbs** (bay & fenugreek leaves)
9 **Oil, butter & ghee**
10 **Coconut** (milk & desiccated)

Lentil types (pages 200–201):

1 **Brown lentils**
2 **Black-eyed beans** (lobia)
3 **Split moong daal**
4 **Yellow lentils** (toor daal)
5 **Whole black urad beans**
6 **Yellow split peas** (channa daal)
7 **Pink lentils** (masoor daal)
8 **White lentils** (urad daal)
9 **Pigeon pea lentils** (loose toor daal)
10 **Dried marrowfat peas**
11 **Puy lentils**

Spice Box

1 Red chilli (dried, crushed & powder)
2 Fennel seeds
3 Cinnamon (sticks & ground)
4 Saffron (threads)
5 Cumin (seeds & ground)
6 Cardamom (pods & ground)
7 Ground turmeric
8 Coriander (seeds & ground)
9 Nutmeg (whole & ground or grated)
10 Black mustard seeds

I

BREAKFAST
- & -
BRUNCH

*

South-Indian-style porridge
Uppma

Known as uppuma, or uppma (as we often pronounce it), this is an Indian breakfast that can also be used as an alternative to polenta. Normally made with semolina, cornmeal or ground bulgur wheat, this recipe is slightly different. Later on in this chapter (see page 23) I have given a more traditional recipe for you to try.

1   Place the oats in a dry frying pan and toast them gently over a low heat until crisp. Transfer to a bowl and wipe the pan clean.

2   Heat the pan and add the oil, heating until hot and it forms a haze. Drop in a couple of mustard seeds and when they start to pop and form tiny bubbles around them, add the rest. Keep a loose cover over the pan to stop the oil from splattering, and as soon as the mustard seeds crackle, add the lentils and cumin seeds.

3   When the lentils colour, add the curry leaves, ginger and green chilli and sauté for a few seconds. Add the onion and cook for about 5 minutes or until it turns pale, then add the nuts and sauté for a couple of minutes until they get a bit of colour.

4   Now mix in the oats. Sauté for a minute or so and add the carrot and squash or pumpkin. Stir for a minute or two, pour in 300ml (10fl oz) water and let it come to the boil. A real uppma should thicken to a polenta consistency, but if you like it thinner and more similar to a porridge, then add more water.

5   When very nearly at the consistency that you like, add the green peas and season to taste.

Serves 4–5

Rolled porridge oats
    10–12 tablespoons
Oil 2 tablespoons
Black mustard seeds ½ teaspoon
White lentils (urad daal) or yellow
    split peas (channa daal)
    1 tablespoon
Cumin seeds ½ heaped teaspoon
Curry leaves 6–8, preferably fresh,
    thinly shredded; if using dried,
    soak in water for 10–12 minutes,
    and dry thoroughly before
    shredding
Fresh ginger 5cm (2in) piece,
    peeled and finely chopped
Fresh green chillies 2 finger-type,
    cut into 5mm (¼ in) pieces
Red onion 1, chopped
Diced mixed nuts 2 tablespoons
Carrot 1, finely diced
Squash or pumpkin small piece,
    finely diced
Green peas 4 tablespoons,
    if fresh blanch (see page 23)
    if frozen add directly
Salt

Baby spinach & fenugreek fritters
Palak methi na muthya

These fritters are full of iron and nutrients and, when eaten with a cup of tea in the morning, they will fill you up and get you ready for the day. Mixing the spinach with the fenugreek mellows the taste of the fenugreek and makes for a very enjoyable breakfast or snack. Classically the fritters are steamed, but in this easier version they are fried. Serve with a sweetish chutney or a tamarind sauce.

1   To make the fritters, wash and chop the spinach and fenugreek leaves as finely as you can and drain them well in a colander.

2   Place the well-drained leaves in a large bowl with all of the fritter ingredients, except for the oil, and mix into a dough.

3   Heat the oil in a large frying pan and, working in batches of about 4 or 5 (depending on the size of your pan), add large tablespoon dollops of the mixture, flattening slightly. Cook over a medium heat for a 2–3 minutes on each side, until golden. Once ready, place on a serving plate.

4   To make the garnish, heat the oil and, when hot, add the mustard seeds, reducing the heat at the same time, and let them pop (hold a loose lid over the frying pan to prevent the seeds from popping all over the place and the oil from splattering). Once the popping reduces, add the sesame seeds. As soon as the seeds change colour, turn off the heat and add the asafoetida, if using. Stir well and then spread the fried seeds over the fritters. Sprinkle over the coriander and serve.

Makes 20–25 fritters

For the fritters
Baby spinach 200g (7oz)
Fresh fenugreek 100g (3½ oz)
   (or spinach, sorrel leaves or kale)
Wholemeal flour 2 tablespoons
Chickpea (gram) flour
   4–5 tablespoons
Finely chopped fresh ginger
   1 heaped teaspoon
Fresh green chillies 1–2, finely
   chopped
Cumin seeds 1 teaspoon, crushed
Lime juice 2 teaspoons
Sugar 1 heaped teaspoon
Bicarbonate of soda ½ teaspoon
Salt ½–1 teaspoon
Oil 2 tablespoons

For the garnish
Oil 1–2 tablespoons
Black mustard seeds 1 teaspoon
White sesame seeds 2 teaspoons
Asafoetida ¼ teaspoon (optional)
Fresh coriander, roughly chopped

Green marrowfat pea bhaji
Watanyachi paatul bhaji

The term 'bhaji' typically represents cooked vegetables and spinach, but this is a great pea preparation. It can be eaten with rice, bread, poori or paav, or sprinkled with Bombay mix and eaten as a snack. In Goa, this is a breakfast staple in vegetarian cafés, where it is served from 6.00am. Around the temples in Goa you will find many variations with different flavours to discover.

1   Soak the peas overnight if possible. Marrowfat peas are very hard and 8–10 hours of soaking will ensure they cook better and faster.

2   Wash the soaked peas, then put them in a pan of salted water to simmer for 30–45 minutes until completely soft. Skim off any scum as it comes to the surface. Once the frothing on the surface stops, stir in the turmeric and add the butter, if using.

3   Meanwhile, heat the oil in a frying pan, add the onion and sauté over a medium heat for about 5 minutes or until it turns pale. Add the garlic and ginger and sauté for 2–3 minutes. Add the red chilli powder and tomato and cook until soft, about 5 minutes, then add the potato, mix well and add a little salt and some water.

4   Once boiling, cover the pan and cook over a medium heat for 20–30 minutes until the potato is cooked but not mushy. Add the garam masala and continue cooking for a minute or so.

5   If the peas are now well cooked and disintegrating, add the contents of the frying pan and stir in well. Add the coconut milk and simmer for 3–4 minutes.

6   Season and squeeze over the lime just before serving, sprinkled with fresh coriander.

Serves 4

Dried green or white marrowfat peas 250g (9oz)
Ground turmeric ½ teaspoon
Butter a knob (optional)
Oil 2 tablespoons
Onion 1, finely chopped
Garlic 2–3 cloves, finely crushed or chopped
Fresh ginger 5cm (2in) piece, peeled and finely chopped
Red chilli powder 1 heaped teaspoon
Tomato 1, finely diced
Potatoes 2, peeled and roughly diced into 1cm (½in) pieces
Garam masala (see page 186) 1 teaspoon
Coconut milk 100ml (3½fl oz)
Lime juice 1 teaspoon
Salt and freshly ground black pepper
Chopped fresh coriander to serve

Mysore bhaji

This is a typical Mysore-style potato bhaji used for filling dosas (crisp rice and lentil pancakes). I haven't included dosas in this book as it isn't a simple recipe, but this bhaji is very versatile and can be served with hot chapattis or poori, rolled in a tortilla, used to fill a samosa or even stuffed into a grilled cheese sandwich.

1   Boil the potatoes in a pan of salted water for 15–20 minutes until soft, then peel and cut into (2cm/¾in) pieces.

2   Heat the oil in a saucepan or casserole dish and when the oil is hot, add the mustard seeds and keep a loose lid over the pan to prevent the seeds from spitting. A few seconds later, add the curry leaves, the ginger, garlic and green chilli and sauté until the garlic starts to change colour, about 2–3 minutes. Add the onion and sauté until it goes soft and pale, about 5 minutes, then add the potato and turmeric.

3   Pour in a little water and cook well for 3–4 minutes until the potato breaks up and gets a bit mushy. Season, add a good drizzle of lime juice, mix in the coriander and serve with the fiery red chutney.

Serves 4

Potatoes 800g (1lb 12oz)
Oil 3 tablespoons
Black mustard seeds 1 teaspoon
Curry leaves 12–15, preferably fresh, shredded; if using dried, soak in water for 10–12 minutes, and dry thoroughly before shredding
Finely chopped fresh ginger 2 teaspoons
Finely chopped garlic 2 teaspoons
Fresh green chillies 2 finger-type, chopped
Onions 2, sliced
Ground turmeric 2 teaspoons
Chopped fresh coriander 2 tablespoons, plus extra to serve
Salt
Lime juice
Hot red chutney (see page 180) to serve

Uppma of mung bean glass noodles, beetroot & potato
Mung seviyan chukunder aur aloo ka uppma

I grew up next to a couple who had fled Burma during the Japanese occupation and one of the things Aunty Bachoo made me was 'chaazaan', or 'fun zae' as her husband pronounced it. It was a Burmese-style uppma, which came served with a plethora of condiments to make a simple dish taste awesome. Today mung bean vermicelli is widely available so I encourage you to experiment.

1   Soak the coconut in a small bowl with just enough water to cover. After about 45 minutes, drain through a sieve. Place the vermicelli in a bowl and pour over boiling water to cover. Let soak for 5 minutes or so, then drain and set aside.

2   Heat the oil in a wok or deep pan and when hot, add the mustard seeds and cover with a lid. As soon as the seeds splutter, add the crushed yellow split peas, cumin seeds, the green chilli, curry leaves and ginger and sauté for a minute or until the broken peas change colour, then remove with a slotted spoon into a small bowl.

3   Add the peanuts to the pan and cook for 3–4 minutes, until lightly browned, then place into the same bowl.

4   Add the onion to the pan and sauté until soft and pale, about 5 minutes. When soft and pale, add the turmeric and sauté for 30 seconds, then add the drained coconut and sauté until the coconut becomes fragrant and slightly coloured. Add the vegetables.

5   Sauté for a minute or two, stirring well, then add the contents of the initial frying pan with the peanuts. Mix and sauté for a few minutes until completely heated through.

6   With scissors, cut the vermicelli into pieces and add to the mix. Stir until well coated and mixed together. Once heated through, taste, season and add a sprinkle of sugar. Lastly, add the fresh coriander, the lime juice and a sprinkle of desiccated coconut and serve.

Serves 4–5

Desiccated coconut 3 tablespoons, plus extra to serve
Mung bean vermicelli 1 x 250g (9oz) pack
Oil 3–4 tablespoons
Black mustard seeds 1 teaspoon
Yellow split peas (channa daal) 2 tablespoons, lightly crushed and any powder strained out
Cumin seeds ½ teaspoon
Fresh green chillies 2–3 finger-type, sliced
Curry leaves 10–12, preferably fresh, shredded; if using dried, soak in water for 10–12 minutes, and dry thoroughly before shredding
Fresh ginger 5cm (2in) piece, peeled and finely chopped
Raw peanuts 2–3 tablespoons
Onions 2 small, finely chopped
Ground turmeric ¼ teaspoon
Beetroot 1 large, baked, peeled and chopped
Potato 1 medium–large, peeled, diced and blanched (see below)
Green peas 2–3 tablespoons, blanched (see below)
Green pepper 1 small, chopped
Sugar a little to sprinkle
Chopped fresh coriander 2 tablespoons
Lime juice 1–2 teaspoons
Salt and freshly ground black pepper

Note
To blanch vegetables, place them in a pot of boiling water for 2–3 minutes then drain and submerge in iced water.

Bulgur & vegetable khichree
Daliya athwa thuli ni khichdi

While it might not sound like an Indian food, bulgur wheat is actually very common, especially in the villages and the wheat-growing regions of India, where there is an abundance of broken wheat and bulgur is a staple for many. Bulgur is low on the glycemic index, so it is nourishing and very filling. A 'khichdi' or 'khichree', which the word 'kedgeree' comes from, is usually cooked with rice and lentils. Here bulgur is used and you have the lentils to bring balance. Serve with some fried or roasted papads (poppadums) and a sweetish chutney.

1   Wash the bulgur, drain and repeat until the water runs clean. Soak for 1 hour, then boil in enough water to cover for 20–25 minutes until cooked but not too soft. Drain and set aside.

2   Wash the rice and mung beans, mix them together, then soak for about 30–40 minutes. Drain.

3   Mix the red chilli powder, ground turmeric, coriander and cumin together in a small bowl. Add some water to make a thin masala paste, then keep covered until needed.

4   Preheat the oven to 130°C/260°F/Gas Mark ¾.

5   Heat the oil in an ovenproof saucepan or casserole dish until hot, but not smoking or hazy. Add the green chilli, ginger and garlic and sauté until the garlic just changes colour, about 2–3 minutes. Add the red onion and sauté until it turns pale, about 5 minutes, then pour in the masala paste, adding a little water to clean the bowl into the pan.

6   When the liquid dries out, add the tomato, carrot and parsnip and cook for 3–4 minutes. Add the spinach and peas, sauté for 30 seconds, then add the drained rice and mung beans.

7   Sauté for a minute, pour in the water, season and cover with a lid. Place on the centre rack of the oven and cook for 15 minutes. Remove and add the cooked bulgur, mix well, season and taste. This khichree is supposed to be a bit wet rather than dry; you may need to put it back into the oven for a few minutes to heat through. Turn the oven off and leave the pan for a few minutes before serving with a blob of butter or ghee on top, if you like.

Serves 4

Bulgur (thuli) 200g (7oz)
Rice 100g (3½oz) (use any type except for glutinous rice such as jasmine or risotto)
Split mung beans (mung daal) 150g (5½oz)
Red chilli powder 1 teaspoon
Ground turmeric ½ teaspoon
Ground coriander 1 tablespoon
Ground cumin 1 tablespoon
Oil 2–3 tablespoons
Fresh green chillies 1–2 finger-type, finely chopped
Fresh ginger 5cm (2in) piece, peeled and finely chopped
Garlic 4–5 cloves, chopped
Red onion 1, chopped
Tomatoes 2, chopped
Carrot 1 small, chopped
Parsnip 1 small, chopped
Fresh spinach leaves 1 handful, chopped or shredded
Green peas 150g (5½oz)
Water 500ml (18 fl oz)
Salt
Butter or ghee to serve (optional)

Breakfast fudge with poppy seeds & almonds
Gol papdi or gor papri

Gol papdi or gor papri is similar to a fudge or halva and makes the perfect mid-morning snack. 'Gol' or 'gor' means 'jaggery', or raw cane sugar, but if you can't find any then use dark brown or muscovado sugar instead. I was fed this as a child during the cold, dry winter months when I lived with my uncle in Rajasthan. It kept us going all day and the slow release of energy saved us from mischief.

1   Heat the ghee in a saucepan or wok over a low–medium heat, add the flour and sauté until evenly browned to a light golden colour.

2   Add the cardamom seeds, coconut and almonds and cook until the flour turns a deep-golden colour. Keep on a low heat as the flour can easily burn.

3   Meanwhile, grease a small 15 x 15cm (6 x 6in) baking tray with some ghee and sprinkle over the poppy seeds to cover the bottom. Add any leftover poppy seeds to the flour mixture and reduce the heat to as low as possible.

4   Grate the jaggery, if using. Turn off the heat and slowly stir the jaggery or sugar in with the nutmeg until fully dissolved and well mixed together. Pour the mixture into the prepared baking tray and smooth out to the edges. Before it sets, mark and cut into 3cm (1¼in) square pieces, then let the tray cool completely.

5   Unmould once set and serve with hot milk or tea.

Makes 16–20 pieces

Ghee 3 tablespoons, plus extra for greasing
Wholemeal flour 300g (10½oz)
Green cardamom pods 2–3, seeds gently toasted and crushed
Desiccated coconut 1 heaped tablespoon
Unskinned almonds 2 tablespoons, chopped
White poppy seeds 2 tablespoons
Jaggery, raw cane, dark brown or muscovado sugar 125–130g (4½oz)
Grated nutmeg a few pinches

Note
You can also add sultanas, pistachios or cashew nuts.

2
EGGS

❋

Old-Ceylon-spiced omelette kaari
Ceylon paarampariya masala muttai curry

Kaari is how one would pronounce the word curry! Kaari or curry represents anything either with or in a sauce predominantly made using coconut milk. Mostly only people from South to South East Asia will use the term curry, as traditionally they use coconut milk. Curry in British terminology denotes everything representing Indian cuisine, which is confusing to those of us who were brought up on curry and rice, as it has a completely different meaning.

1   Heat the oil in a pan over a medium heat and add the ginger, garlic paste, green chilli and curry leaves.

2   Sauté for 2–3 minutes, until the garlic changes colour, and add the onion.

3   Meanwhile, in a small bowl, mix together the curry powder, chilli powder and turmeric with 5–6 tablespoons of water to form a smooth paste. Set aside.

4   After 6–7 minutes, or when the onions turn a light brown, add the curry paste and cook on a medium to low flame until the liquid dries out and you can see oil emerging.

5   Add the tomatoes and cook for 10 minutes or until the mixture has reduced and looks almost like jam, then add the coconut milk and simmer for 10–15 minutes until it is the consistency of fresh double cream. Add some seasoning.

6   Meanwhile, make the omelettes. Melt the butter in a frying pan and add the cashews. Sauté until they change colour, about 2–3 minutes, remove with a slotted spoon and let drain on some kitchen paper. Now add the onions to the same pan and cook for 3–4 minutes, until pale brown. Take off the heat and strain the onions in a colander (with a bowl underneath to collect the butter). Squeeze well to get rid of any moisture.

7   Beat the eggs in a bowl, stir through the onions, tomatoes and coriander and season well.

8   Wipe the frying pan dry and heat half the strained butter over a medium heat. As the butter begins to froth, add half the beaten egg mixture. Once one side is cooked, about 2 minutes, flip to cook through and then remove once just cooked (it will continue to cook in the curry). Slice into strips and repeat with the remaining mixture.

9   Add the omelette strips and cashews to the warm curry sauce, top with the coriander and serve immediately.

Serves 4–5

Rapeseed oil 3 tablespoons
Ginger & garlic paste (see page 188) 2 level tablespoons
Fresh green chillies 2–3, slit lengthways
Curry leaves 10–12, preferably fresh, thinly shredded; if using dried, soak in water for 10–12 minutes, and dry thoroughly before shredding
Red onions 3 medium, finely chopped
Hot madras curry powder (see page 193) 2 teaspoons
Red chilli powder 2 teaspoons
Ground turmeric ½ teaspoon
Tomatoes 4–5 medium, chopped
Coconut milk 700–800ml (1¼–1⅓ pints)
Fresh coriander 6–8 sprigs, stalks and leaves chopped, plus extra for serving
Salt and freshly ground black pepper

For the omelettes
Butter 2 tablespoons
Cashew nuts 2–3 tablespoons
Red onions 2 small, chopped
Eggs 6–8
Tomatoes 2 medium, chopped
Fresh coriander 6–8 sprigs, stalks and leaves chopped

Masala omelette wrapped in chapatti
Rotli ma masala aamlet

A masala omelette is a very popular Parsee snack, either rolled up in a chapatti or made into a sandwich. Hot or cold, it tastes just as good, so is perfect for taking on picnics. It tastes even better when served with the spicy tomato sauce on page 192.

1   Beat the eggs in a bowl and mix through all the other ingredients for the omelette, except for the oil.

2   Place a frying pan over a medium heat and add a teaspoon of oil.

3   When the oil starts to smoke, add roughly one sixth of the egg mixture and tilt the pan to spread it over the bottom. Allow it to brown on one side, about 2 minutes, then flip it over. Be sure to let it colour well on both sides, then remove to a plate. Repeat with the remaining mixture.

4   Dampen a clean tea towel and place the chapattis inside. Fold over the towel so that the breads are completely covered and place in the microwave for 15–20 seconds to soften. The breads need to be pliable for wrapping the omelettes.

5   Place each omelette on top of a heated chapatti and, if you like, sprinkle over some sugar and a drizzle of lime or lemon juice. Roll up and slightly heat each roll in a griddle or frying pan. Serve with a generous helping of butter and enjoy.

Makes 6

Eggs 6
Onions 2 small, finely chopped
Ground turmeric ½ teaspoon
Ground coriander 1 heaped
    teaspoon
Ground cumin ½ teaspoon
Red chilli powder ¾ teaspoon
Fresh green chillies 2, chopped
Chopped fresh coriander
    1–2 heaped tablespoons
Oil 2–3 tablespoons
Salt

To finish
Chapattis 6, shop-bought or
    homemade (see page 199)
Sugar 2–3 teaspoons (optional)
Lime or lemon juice from ½ lime
    or lemon (optional)
Butter

Note
Butter can also be spread on the inside of each chapatti before adding the omelette. Tomato ketchup is a great addition too.

Spiced aubergine & tomato frittata
Baked brinjal kookoo bademjaan

The Persians, so far as history tells us, were the original creators of what we know as a Spanish omelette or the frittata, which is part of the great Persian heritage to Middle Eastern, Middle Asian and European cuisines. Little wonder then that we Parsees love our eggs and can eat them 24/7. This frittata is derived from a classic, but I have added a bit of a twist to it, so any die-hard Persian ladies, do please forgive my insolence.

1   Preheat your oven to 200°C/400°F/Gas Mark 6.

2   Poke several holes in the aubergines, either using a fork or a thin knife. Rub them with oil, place on a baking tray and bake on the top shelf of the oven for 25–30 minutes until soft throughout.

3   Transfer to a colander and place it over a bowl to catch any liquid. Let cool completely. Reduce the temperature to 180°C/350°F/Gas Mark 4.

4   Once the aubergine is cold, peel and discard the skins, then finely chop. Set aside in a bowl.

5   Heat the oil in a large frying pan and sauté the onion until it turns light brown, roughly 3–4 minutes. Add the green chilli, garlic and leek and sauté for 10–12 minutes, until the leek is soft and cooked through. Add the spring onion, red pepper, turmeric and chilli powders and sauté for 1–2 minutes. Add the aubergine and sauté for another 2–3 minutes, then add the walnuts for a minute, then switch off the heat.

6   In a large bowl, break the eggs and beat lightly. Add the flour and mix until combined, then add the coriander and the sautéed ingredients. Stir well and season.

7   Grease a 20 x 30cm (8 x 12 in) baking dish with oil and pour the mix into it, levelling it out evenly. Arrange the sliced tomato on top so that the entire area is covered and drizzle over some oil.

8   Cover the dish loosely with some foil or a lid and bake, covered, for 15–20 minutes. Remove the foil or lid, top with the grated cheese and return to the oven for another 10–15 minutes or until the tomatoes are well browned, the cheese has melted and the dish has set. Serve hot, warm or even cold.

Serves 4–6

Aubergines 4–5 large or 6 medium
Extra-virgin olive or rapeseed oil 2–3 tablespoons, plus extra for greasing and baking
Onion 1, thinly sliced
Fresh green chillies 2–3 finger-type, finely chopped
Garlic 2–3 cloves, finely chopped
Leek 1, thinly sliced
Spring onions 2–3, thinly sliced
Red pepper 1, finely diced
Ground turmeric ½ teaspoon
Red chilli powder ½ teaspoon
Walnuts 2–3 tablespoons, chopped
Eggs 3–4
Plain flour 2 heaped tablespoons
Fresh coriander 15–20 sprigs, stalks and leaves finely chopped
Tomatoes 3–4, cut into 3mm (⅛in) thick slices
Vegetarian hard cheese 30g (1oz), grated
Salt and freshly ground black pepper

Note
To add to the magic, top with vegetarian feta cheese.

Bombay-style masala French toast

Bombay is notorious for copying different styles from various regions of the world and then adapting them to suit its palate. Eating sandwiches on the pavements of Bombay is part and parcel of our city's culture, and the Bombay sandwich is well known among Indians. Anyway, here goes, and my sincere apologies if any French people cringe at the thought of this.

1   Preheat the oven to 140°C/275°F/Gas Mark 1.

2   Beat the eggs in a bowl and add in all the ingredients except for the oil, butter, bread and cheese. Stir until well combined.

3   Heat a non-stick frying pan and add a little less than a teaspoon of the oil and some butter and let the two melt. When the butter bubbles and heats up, stir the eggs, take a slice of the bread and dip the whole slice into the egg mixture.

4   Remove from the egg mixture, and place the slice in the frying pan. Let cook until lightly browned, about 3–4 minutes, then flip over and cook until the other side is brown. If not enough of the other ingredients in the egg mixture have stuck to the slice, spoon some onto the cooked side and flip to cook again. Once cooked, place each slice on a baking tray and repeat with the remaining slices of bread, oil and butter.

5   Once all six slices are done, sprinkle the cheese over the top and place in the oven until the cheese has melted, about 4–5 minutes.

6   Serve hot with some tomato ketchup and chilli sauce.

Makes 6

Eggs 3–4
Onion 1, very finely chopped
Plum tomato 1, very finely chopped
Fresh green chillies 2–3 finger-
   type, finely chopped
Fresh coriander leaves
   2 tablespoons, finely chopped,
   plus extra to serve
Ground turmeric ¼ teaspoon
Red chilli powder ½ teaspoon
Cumin seeds ½ teaspoon, finely
   crushed
Single cream or full-fat milk
   100ml (3½fl oz)
Oil 2 tablespoons
Butter 3–4 tablespoons
Bread 6 thick slices
Cheese 100g (3½oz), finely grated
Freshly ground black pepper
   ½ teaspoon
Salt

> **Note**
> Cut these into squares and
> serve as a canapé.
>   You can make them in
> advance and store in a
> container in the fridge for
> up to 2 days. Reheat in the
> oven before serving.

Deep-fried boiled egg in a chickpea batter
Egg bonda

A bonda, or wada as it is usually called outside of southern India, is something that has been dipped in a batter and fried. Unlike pakoras, which are generally smaller pieces eaten as a plateful, the bonda is something large and whole and eaten as a full snack or, for many, as a meal stuffed into a bun. The eggs are delicious served with some chutney or a dip. Ketchup also goes well and you can serve in a soft roll too, if you like.

1   Preheat the oven to 140°C/275°F/Gas Mark 1.

2   Boil the eggs for 7 minutes, then turn off the heat and let rest in the hot water for 1 minute before draining. Cover with iced water to cool.

3   Sift the flours, chilli and turmeric powders and salt into a bowl.

4   In a separate large bowl, mix together the cumin, green chillies, ginger & garlic paste and the onion. Add the spiced flour mixture and stir well to combine. Add in a little cold water, as needed, to make the batter a consistency between single and double cream.

5   Heat 2cm (½ in) oil in a deep pan over a medium–high heat, until hot.

6   Remove the shells from the eggs. Dip an egg in the plain flour, then roll it in the batter and very gently immerse it in the hot oil. Be very careful when doing this, don't drop it in as the hot oil will splatter. Cook for 30 seconds then remove with a slotted spoon and place on a baking tray lined with kitchen paper. Repeat with the remaining eggs.

7   Pat the eggs dry with kitchen paper. Dip them in the batter again and carefully fry for another 30 seconds or so. Again, remove from the oil using a slotted spoon and place on another baking tray. These eggs can sometimes burst if they cool down too quickly, so it is best to keep them in a warmed oven (for no longer than 5–6 minutes) while you cook the remaining eggs. Serve immediately.

Serves 4–5 as a snack

Eggs 4–5
Chickpea (gram) flour 200g (7oz)
Rice flour or cornflour
    2–3 tablespoons
Red chilli powder ½ teaspoon
Ground turmeric ½ teaspoon
Salt ½ teaspoon
Cumin seeds ¼ teaspoon, crushed
Fresh green chillies 1–2 finger-
    type, finely chopped
Ginger & garlic paste (see page
    188) ½ teaspoon
Onion 1 small, very finely chopped
Oil for deep-frying
Plain flour for dusting
Fresh coriander to serve (optional)

Note
To make pakoras, boil the eggs for 8–9 minutes, then cut each egg into three or four slices and coat and fry individually.

Masala omelette in a Goan-style curry sauce
Goan-style ros omelette

Pronounced 'roas', 'ros' simply means 'sauce' and is made from a base of onions, tomatoes and coconut milk. Traditionally the omelette is placed on top of the ros and eaten with hot fresh poori, chapattis or the famous Goan poi – a sourdough roll. Below is a straightforward recipe and the sauce is adaptable to other uses too – add vegetables or boiled eggs to it and use it to make a simple curry. Pictured overleaf.

1   To make the sauce, heat the oil in a saucepan over a medium heat, add the onion and sauté until pale, about 3–4 minutes. Add the curry leaves and the ginger & garlic paste and cook for 1–2 minutes.

2   Mix the turmeric and red chilli powders with 4–5 tablespoons water to make a paste and add to the saucepan. Sauté for about a minute or until the liquid dries out, then add the tomato, cover the pan and simmer for 6–8 minutes until the tomato is cooked.

3   Add the garam masala and stir in the coconut milk. Simmer, covered, for 4–5 minutes and then season well.

4   Meanwhile, make the omelette. Heat 1 teaspoon of oil in a non-stick frying pan over a medium heat until just smoking.

5   Beat the eggs in a bowl, add some seasoning and stir in the green chilli and coriander.

6   Pour in a quarter of the egg mixture. Tilt the pan to spread the mixture over the bottom of the pan and let it rest for 30 seconds. Keep an eye to make sure that it is not burning, then flip the omelette over for just a few seconds and transfer to a large plate. Fold into quarters. Repeat with the remaining oil and egg mixture.

7   Pour the hot curry sauce over the top of the omelettes and serve immediately with extra coriander and some rice, if you would like.

Serves 4

Oil 2 tablespoons
Onion 1, finely chopped
Curry leaves 6–8, preferably fresh, thinly shredded; if using dried, soak in water for 10–12 minutes, and dry thoroughly before shredding
Ginger & garlic paste (see page 188) 2 teaspoons
Ground turmeric ½ teaspoon
Red chilli powder 1 teaspoon
Tomatoes 2 large, chopped
Garam masala (see page 186) ¼ teaspoon
Coconut milk 200–250ml (7–9fl oz)
Salt and freshly ground black pepper

For the omelettes
Oil 4 teaspoons
Eggs 8
Fresh green chillies 4–6 finger-type, finely chopped
Fresh coriander leaves 4–5 tablespoons, chopped, plus extra for serving

Keralan-style egg curry
Mutta aviyal

A light Keralan-style curry with eggs, this is great when served with other vegetarian dishes, rice or even noodles.

1   Boil the potatoes until cooked and soft, about 15 minutes. Drain, peel and cut into wedges. Boil the eggs for 7–8 minutes, then cool rapidly in iced water. Once cool, drain and carefully remove the shells.

2   Place the coconut, onion, chilli and turmeric powders in a blender and blitz to a smooth paste.

3   Heat the oil in a large saucepan and add the cumin, curry leaves and green chillies. Sauté until the cumin changes colour, about 2 minutes, then pour the paste into the pan along with some water.

4   Let simmer for 15–20 minutes, keeping an eye on the pan to make sure that the mixture does not become too thick, and add more water as needed. If it begins to pop and splutter, add a little water. Once the raw onion flavour has disappeared, add the potato and boiled eggs to heat through for 5 minutes. Season well and serve with some rice and popadoms.

Serves 4

Potatoes 2
Eggs 8
Freshly grated coconut or desiccated coconut 250g (9oz) or 200g (7oz), desiccated soaked in 400–500ml (14–18fl oz) hot water for 1 hour and drained
Red onion 1, chopped
Red chilli powder 1 heaped teaspoon
Ground turmeric ½ teaspoon
Oil 2 tablespoons
Cumin seeds 1 heaped teaspoon
Curry leaves 15–20, preferably fresh, thinly shredded; if using dried, soak in water for 10–12 minutes, and dry thoroughly before shredding
Fresh green chillies 4–5 finger-type, slit lengthways
Salt

Note
If you like, you can add more in-season diced vegetables at the end of step 3.

Indian fried egg toast
Eggs Kejriwal

I had to put this recipe in, even though mine varies from the original, created by a chef named Kejriwal. It is more or less a variation of Bombay's famous Chilli Cheese Toast and is sold in more places now than the creator could ever have envisaged. You will notice that it is served with ketchup. Most Indians love to be served ketchup with omelettes and other kinds of egg preparations, including fried eggs. Don't ask me where that love came from, but it's there.

1   Heat the butter in a non-stick frying pan over a medium heat. Once the butter has melted, add the onion and sauté until soft, about 3–4 minutes, then set aside to cool.

2   Toast the slices of bread lightly, spread with some butter and place on a small baking tray.

3   In a bowl, mix together the cooled onion, cheese, mustard, coriander, green chilli and one of the eggs. Blend together well.

4   Spread this cheese mixture on top of each slice of toast and grill under a medium heat for 4–5 minutes, or until set and bubbling.

5   Meanwhile, wipe the non-stick frying pan clean, add the oil and heat until nearly smoking. Fry the remaining eggs for a couple of minutes, so that the white is set and there is still a lovely runny yolk.

6   As soon as the toasts are grilled, transfer to two plates, top with an egg, season and serve with ketchup, if desired.

Serves 2 as a snack

Salted butter 1 teaspoon, plus 1 heaped tablespoon for the toast
Onion 1 small, finely chopped
Bread 2 thick slices
Mature Cheddar 150g (5½oz), grated
Hot English mustard 2 teaspoons
Fresh coriander leaves 1–2 tablespoons, chopped
Fresh green chillies 1–2 finger-type, finely chopped
Eggs 3
Oil 1 tablespoon
Salt and freshly ground black pepper
Tomato ketchup to serve (optional)

Masala scrambled eggs with paneer
Chaarvaela enda saathay narum paneer

The Parsee love for eggs simply knows no bounds. Everyone's mother makes the best scrambled eggs or akoori or whatever, so it is time to build your own reputation and enjoy one of God's greatest creations... eggs!

1   Melt the butter and oil in a saucepan over a medium heat. When the butter begins to froth, add the cumin seeds and, in a few seconds, the onion.

2   Sauté the onion for 4–5 minutes or until it turns pale and goes soft, then add the ginger, garlic and green chilli and sauté for a couple of minutes over a low–medium heat.

3   Meanwhile, beat the eggs in a bowl. And place your bread in the toaster.

4   As soon as the garlic changes colour, add the coriander and the paneer. Mix well and add in the eggs. For a really soft, runny scrambled egg, you need to stir continuously over a low–medium heat. Cook until you see the liquid start to thicken and it has a very soft, runny consistency. Turn off the heat but continue stirring and add the pepper. The heat from the pan will continue to cook the eggs.

5   Butter the toast and, once happy with the consistency, simply pile the scrambled eggs on top of the toast and serve with extra paneer crumbled over.

Serves 4

Butter 2 heaped tablespoons, plus extra for the toast
Oil 1 teaspoon
Cumin seeds ½ teaspoon
Red onion 1, finely chopped
Fresh ginger 2.5cm (1in) piece, peeled and finely chopped
Garlic 2 cloves, finely chopped
Fresh green chillies 2–3, finely chopped
Eggs 6–8
Bread 4 slices
Chopped fresh coriander 2 heaped tablespoons
Soft paneer 200g (7oz) (see page 190), (or use finely grated hard paneer or mild Cheddar), plus extra to serve
Freshly ground black pepper ¼ teaspoon

Note
If you are someone who makes whey ricotta or masacarpone at home, then you can use this instead of the paneer. It should be soft, but drained well.

You can also split full-fat hot milk with some live culture yogurt. Keep stirring gently until it splits well, then pass through a fine muslin cloth placed inside a sieve and drain thoroughly. The whey can be used to make bread, or add a little seasoning and drink when cold.

Andhra-style poached egg curry

The food from the Andhra region, of which the city of Hyderabad is the capital, is probably the hottest in India. This egg curry is not that spicy, but if anyone from Andhra made this, then naturally the chillies would be doubled or even trebled. The level of heat is left to your discretion, though you should be a bit adventurous, and keep some yogurt ready on the side. This light and delicious curry can be eaten with rice or chapattis.

1   Preheat your oven to 130°C/260°F/Gas Mark ¾.

2   Place the fenugreek leaves on a baking tray in the oven and turn the oven off. Leave the fenugreek to toast for at least 30 minutes, then crumble finely, removing any large twigs.

3   Heat the oil in a saucepan or a deep frying pan over a medium heat and add the cumin seeds. As soon as they start to change colour, add the ginger & garlic paste and the green chillies. Sauté for 1 minute, then add the onion and cook for 4–5 minutes.

4   Meanwhile, mix the turmeric and chilli powders in a small bowl with approximately 2–3 tablespoons of water in order to make a runny paste. As soon as the onion starts to colour, add the turmeric and chilli water and clean the bowl into the cooking pot. You may need to use a little more water to clean the bowl completely.

5   As the water starts to dry out, the oil will bubble and reappear at the bottom of the pan, signifying that the chilli powder is cooking. Keep the heat at medium, add the tomatoes and cook for about 5 minutes or until the whole mixture has thickened.

6   Stir in the coconut milk and bring to the boil. If you like more sauce, then add a little more water. Turn the heat down to low. Season the mixture and add most of the coriander. Break the eggs into the sauce one by one. The eggs will slowly poach and they are ready once the whites are no longer translucent, about 4–5 minutes on a simmer.

7   Sprinkle over the garam masala and the remaining chopped coriander to serve.

Serves 4 with rice

Dried fenugreek leaves (kasuri methi) 1 tablespoon
Oil 2 tablespoons
Cumin seeds 2 teaspoons
Ginger & garlic paste (see page 188) 2 tablespoons
Fresh green chillies 3 finger-type, slit into 4 but not cut through at the stem
Red onions 2, finely chopped
Ground turmeric ½ teaspoon
Red chilli powder 2 heaped teaspoons
Tomatoes 4–5, chopped or 1 x 400g (14oz) tin of chopped tomatoes
Coconut milk 200ml (7fl oz)
Chopped fresh coriander 1½ tablespoons
Eggs 4
Garam masala (see page 186) ¼ teaspoon
Salt

3

SOUPS

❋

Roasted celeriac, leek, potato, turnip & swede soup

The vegetable bounty in Britain is simply amazing. Not only do we get an abundance of British vegetables, but we also receive them from all over the world. Soups are one of the best ways of exploring these vegetables and I enjoy playing with different flavours. This soup has a smooth texture and is very tasty.

1   Preheat the oven to 150°C/300°F/Gas Mark 2.

2   Cut all the vegetables into 1cm (½in) cubes and place in a large bowl.

3   Heat the oil in a casserole dish over a medium heat and when hot, add the sage leaves. Lift them out with a pair of tongs or tweezers in 10–12 seconds and drain on some kitchen paper.

4   In the same oil, fry the coriander, cumin and fennel seeds, bay leaves and garlic and sauté until the garlic changes colour slightly, about 2 minutes. Strain the herbs and spices over the bowl of vegetables, so that the oil coats the vegetables. Set the herbs and spices aside.

5   Transfer the vegetables to a baking tray, sprinkle with salt and combine until well coated. Roast in the oven for about 40 minutes, stirring them after 10–15 minutes. Once well cooked and coloured, remove from the oven and let cool slightly.

6   Add the cooled vegetables to a blender along with the fried coriander, cumin and fennel seeds, but not the bay leaves.

7   Blitz the vegetables, adding the stock as needed to make a smooth purée. Pour into the used casserole dish and add more stock or water to make up a soup consistency.

8   Gradually bring to the boil and add back the bay leaves and the butter, then reduce to a simmer. Taste and season. Grate in some nutmeg while whisking, to ensure it is blended in well. Add the chopped coriander.

9   Serve in bowls, with some cream, if you like, and the fried sage leaves. This is delicious with hot bread rolls and butter, or toasted croutons.

Serves 6

Celeriac 1 small, trimmed and scrubbed well or peeled
Carrots 2 small
Potatoes 2
Turnip 1, trimmed
Swede 1, trimmed
Leek 1, trimmed, split lengthways and washed well
Onion 1 large, sliced
Oil 2 tablespoons
Fresh sage leaves 10–12
Coriander seeds 2 teaspoons
Cumin seeds ½ teaspoon
Fennel seeds ½ teaspoon
Bay leaves 2–3
Garlic 3–4 cloves, sliced
Vegetable stock 1 litre (1¾ pints)
Butter 1 tablespoon
Grated nutmeg
Fresh coriander a few sprigs, chopped
Salt and freshly ground black pepper
Double cream 1 heaped teaspoon for each bowl to serve (optional)

Summer vegetable soup
Gurmee kay mausam ka subz bhara shorba

Summer is the time for a bounty of British homegrown produce, and we should definitely maximize their availability. You should try and work with as many different vegetables, fruits and berries as you can to create some amazing soups, both hot and cold, as well as so much more. Some of the vegetables that make excellent soups are: beetroot, broccoli, butternut or other squashes and pumpkins, carrot, cauliflower, celery, courgette, cucumber, garlic, kale, kohlrabi, leeks, lettuce, peas, marrow, mangetout and potatoes. Pictured overleaf (left).

1 Heat the oil or butter in a deep casserole dish over a medium heat and add the cinnamon stick and cumin seeds. When the cumin seeds begin to change colour, add the spring onion, onion and garlic and sauté until the onions turn pale, about 4–5 minutes.

2 Increase the heat to high, add all the vegetables and sauté for a couple of minutes, then add the stock to cover. Bring the stock to the boil, then turn down the heat to a simmer and cook until soft, about 30 minutes.

3 After 2–3 minutes, check if the broccoli stalks are not too tough and almost cooked. If so, turn off the heat and let the mixture cool.

4 Once cooled, remove the cinnamon stick and blitz to a smooth purée.

5 Return the soup to the casserole dish and bring to a simmer. Season, then mix in the coriander, chives or parsley. To serve, add some cream, whipped seasoned yogurt or a nice dollop of butter and top with a sprinkling of red chilli powder.

Serves 4–5

Oil or butter 2 tablespoons
Cinnamon stick 7.5cm (3in) piece
Cumin seeds 1 teaspoon
Spring onions 2, trimmed and sliced
Onion 1 small, sliced
Garlic 2–3 cloves, sliced
Fresh spinach 30–40 leaves, shredded
Cucumber 1 small, chopped
Lettuce 1 small dense-type (200g/7oz), roughly chopped
Shelled green peas 150–200g (5½–7oz), use fresh or frozen
Broccoli 200–250g (7–9oz), stalks sliced and florets separated
Vegetable stock 750ml–1 litre (1¼–1¾ pints)
Chopped fresh coriander, chives or parsley 1 heaped tablespoon
Salt and freshly ground black pepper
Cream, yogurt or butter to serve
Red chilli powder to serve

Note
Add some coconut milk to the soup to make it creamier – just reduce the amount of vegetable stock accordingly.

Spicy mushroom & celeriac soup
Dhingri or shalari ka soup

A simple soup to make, packed with flavour and taste. You can add some potato, parsnip or other root vegetable to this. The taste won't disappoint. Pictured overleaf (right).

1   Heat the oil in a casserole dish over a medium heat and fry the peppercorns and cinnamon for a few seconds. Add the cumin and coriander seeds and continue cooking until the cumin changes colour, about 1–2 minutes.

2   Add the curry leaves and, once they splutter, the red chilli. A few seconds later add the garlic and vegetables and sauté for 5–6 minutes until all the vegetables are just becoming soft.

3   Add the water, increase the heat and bring the mixture to the boil. Boil for about 30 minutes until all the vegetables are fully cooked. Remove the cinnamon stick and blitz to a smooth purée.

4   Return the soup to the casserole dish and reheat gently. Season, adding the tamarind paste a little at a time and tasting as you go. Stir in the coriander and top with a lacing of cream, if desired, and serve.

Serves 4–6

Oil 2–3 tablespoons
Black peppercorns 3–4
Cinnamon stick 2.5–4cm
   (1–1½in) piece
Cumin seeds 1 teaspoon
Coriander seeds 1 teaspoon
Curry leaves 10–12, preferably
   fresh, thinly shredded; if using
   dried, soak in water for 10–12
   minutes, and dry thoroughly
   before shredding
Dried red chillies 2 large mild-type,
   deseeded and chopped
Garlic 2–3 cloves, sliced
Mushrooms 100–150g (3½–5½oz),
   sliced
Celeriac 1 small or ½ large,
   thickly sliced
Potato 1, thickly sliced
Onion 1, thickly sliced
Fresh coriander 6–8 stalks,
   chopped
Water 1 litre (1¾ pints)
Light Thai tamarind paste
   2 tablespoons
Salt
Cream to serve (optional)

Sweetcorn, celery & coconut chowder with almonds

Naturally, this is a take on the original, but it is a lighter version as it uses coconut milk rather than cream. This is very addictive and the spices make this a wonderfully refreshing and comforting soup, great for when you simply wish to sit and relax.

1 Soak the almonds in the boiling water for about an hour, then drain and place in a blender. Add the coconut milk, 3–4 tablespoons of the sweetcorn along with the water from the tin, and blitz to a purée.

2 Heat the oil in a deep casserole dish over a medium–low heat and add the cumin seeds. As soon as they sizzle and change colour, add the ginger, garlic, onion and green chilli. After 2–3 minutes or as soon as the garlic starts to change colour, add the celery, sweet potato and potato and continue to sauté for 5–6 minutes until they have softened slightly.

3 If using the wine, add it now and let cook until nearly dry. Mix in the remaining sweetcorn and sauté for a minute or so, then add the stock and coriander stalks.

4 Cover the dish, stir regularly and cook on a low boil for 30–35 minutes, until the vegetables are cooked through. Add the puréed almonds and simmer for 3–4 minutes or until the soup thickens a little. Whisk slightly to break up the sweet potato and potato to thicken the texture of the soup, but be careful not to make it smooth.

5 Season and serve with the coriander sprinkled over the top.

Serves 4–5

Ground almonds 2–3 tablespoons
Boiling water 250ml (9fl oz)
Coconut milk 1 x 400ml (14fl oz) tin
Sweetcorn 1 x 340g (12oz) tin
Oil 2 tablespoons
Cumin seeds 1 teaspoon
Fresh ginger 2.5–4cm (1–1½in) piece, peeled and finely chopped
Garlic 3–4 cloves, chopped
Onion 1 small, finely chopped
Fresh green chillies 1–2 finger-type, slit, deseeded and finely chopped
Celery 2 sticks, trimmed and very finely diced
Sweet potato ¼–½, peeled and very finely diced
Potato 1, peeled and very finely diced
White wine 100ml (3½fl oz) (optional)
Vegetable stock 500ml (18fl oz)
Fresh coriander 10–12 stalks, finely chopped, for the soup, plus 1 tablespoon leaves, chopped, for the garnish
Salt and freshly ground black pepper

Mushroom & lentil soup
Mushroom tomato daal russum

Russums are South Indian soups, which always have a slight tang from lime or tamarind. At times they are too tangy for my liking, but they can be delicious. Some russums are simple and others have added extras.

1 Rinse the lentils, then soak in plenty of cold water for an hour or so.

2 In a saucepan over a medium heat, bring the tamarind paste and water gradually to the boil, add the drained lentils and simmer until cooked through. This will take 20 minutes for the pink lentils, 30–35 minutes for the pigeon pea lentils.

3 Gently toast the cumin seeds in a small frying pan over a low heat for a minute or so until aromatic and crisp, then cool and crush in a mortar.

4 Heat the oil in a wok, or a kadhai if you have one, and add the cinnamon, curry leaves, ginger, garlic and green chilli. As soon as the garlic changes colour, about 2–3 minutes, add the onion. After about 5 minutes, or once the onion turns soft and starts to colour, add the tomatoes and the turmeric. Sauté until the tomatoes nearly dry out, about 8–10 minutes, then add the mushrooms and crushed cumin seeds.

5 Sauté for a minute or so then pour in the lentils and add the coriander stalks. Bring to a boil and simmer for 10–15 minutes over a very low heat. Season with salt and pepper. Fold in some coriander leaves just before serving.

Serves 4–5 as an accompaniment

Pink lentils (masoor daal) or pigeon pea lentils 100g (3½oz)
Light Thai tamarind paste 50ml (2fl oz)
Boiling water 1 litre (1¾ pints)
Cumin seeds 1 teaspoon
Oil 2 tablespoons
Cinnamon stick 2.5cm (1in) piece
Curry leaves 12–15 preferably fresh, chopped; if using dried, soak in water for 10–12 minutes, and dry thoroughly before chopping
Fresh ginger 2.5–5cm (1–2in) piece, finely chopped
Garlic 2 cloves, chopped
Fresh green chillies 2 finger-type, sliced
Onions 2 small, roughly chopped
Tomatoes 2–3, chopped
Ground turmeric ½ teaspoon
Mushrooms 150g (5½oz), sliced
Fresh coriander 10–12 stalks, chopped, plus 1 tablespoon leaves, chopped, for the garnish
Salt and freshly ground black pepper

Note
You can also remove the cinnamon and purée the soup. Puréeing will give it a completely different profile and taste. If puréeing, keep a few cooked, sliced mushrooms aside and add as a garnish.

South-Indian-style tomato & garlic soup
Poondu thakkali russum

Russums, the simple, nourishing and healthy soups made in South India, are served as a digestif, a flavour enhancer and to have something to soak the rice into, or as a soup course served before the meal.

1 Rinse and soak the lentils in plenty of cold water for 2–3 hours. Drain, and boil in fresh water for about 25 minutes, or until cooked then purée.

2 Soak the tamarind paste in the boiling water for about 20 minutes. Transfer to a saucepan set over a medium heat and bring the mixture gradually to the boil, adding the turmeric and tomatoes. Stir regularly until cooked through, about 10 minutes.

3 Toast the chillies in a small dry frying pan over a medium heat, stirring regularly. Let cool, then roughly crush in a mortar. Add the crushed chillies to the tamarind water with the cumin seeds, peppercorns, garlic and ginger, along with the lentils, and bring to a simmer.

4 In the same frying pan, heat the oil and add the mustard seeds until they crackle. Do keep a lid ready to prevent the seeds from splattering everywhere. When they begin to pop, add the curry leaves and sauté for a few seconds. Add them both to the soup and bring gradually to a boil.

5 Season the soup and add the chopped coriander. Drop a coriander sprig into each bowl and pour the soup over to serve.

Serves 4–6 as a side

Yellow lentils (toor daal) 3 tablespoons
Light Thai tamarind paste 50ml (2fl oz)
Boiling water 1 litre (1¾ pints)
Ground turmeric ½ teaspoon
Tomatoes 3–4, chopped
Dried red chillies 2–3 large, deseeded
Cumin seeds 1½ teaspoons
Black peppercorns 1 tablespoon
Garlic 5–6 cloves, crushed
Fresh ginger 2.5cm (1in) piece, finely chopped
Oil 1 tablespoon
Black mustard seeds 1 teaspoon
Curry leaves 12–15, preferably fresh, thinly shredded; if using dried, soak in water for 10–12 minutes, and dry thoroughly before shredding
Chopped fresh coriander 1 heaped tablespoon, plus extra sprigs to serve
Salt

Winter vegetable & barley soup

A vegetable soup with a wintry appeal. This makes a nice meal on the weekend with some hot crusty bread and some cheese.

1   Soak the pearl barley in the boiling water for an hour and drain.

2   Preheat the oven to 150°C/300°F/Gas Mark 2.

3   Roast the beetroot and chestnuts for 10–12 minutes, then remove the chestnuts and let cool. Return the beetroot to the oven for another 30–40 minutes until cooked, then let cool. Peel the chestnuts and beetroot and chop into small pieces. Set aside.

4   Cook the soaked barley in plenty of fresh water for 15–20 minutes until done, then drain over a bowl to collect the water for your soup.

5   Heat the butter or oil in a deep casserole dish. Add the cumin seeds, garlic and sage leaves and sauté for a minute or so, then add the shallots.

6   As soon as the shallots are pale and soft, about 4–5 minutes, add the parsnip, swede, leek, cauliflower, squash and the chestnut pieces and sauté for a few minutes, turning regularly.

7   Add the barley water and 500ml (18fl oz) or more of water and bring to a boil. Simmer until the vegetables are cooked and soft, about 20 minutes.

8   Let cool a little before blitzing the soup and the beetroot pieces to a purée. The soup should turn a lovely pink colour.

9   Once puréed, return the soup to the casserole dish and place over a medium heat. Add the drained barley and cook until heated through, but do not let it boil. Season and serve garnished with chopped parsley or coriander, croutons and a dollop of cream, if you like.

Serves 4–5

Pearl barley 150g (5½oz)
Boiling water 500ml (18fl oz)
Beetroot 1 small
Chestnuts 10–12
Butter or olive oil 2 tablespoons
Cumin seeds 1 teaspoon
Garlic 3–4 cloves, chopped
Sage leaves 3
Shallots 2–3, sliced
Parsnip 1 small, scrubbed well and cut into pieces
Swede 1 small, scrubbed well and cut into pieces
Leek 1 small, slit into 4, sliced, soaked in a little cold water and then drained
Cauliflower 1 small, florets and stalks sliced
Butternut squash ⅛, cut into small pieces
Salt and freshly ground black pepper

To serve (optional)
Fresh parsley or coriander, chopped
Croutons
Cream

Roasted beetroot, carrot & sweet potato soup

Beetroot is one amazing vegetable and, in my opinion, grossly underrated. Yes it loses colour when cooked, but if cooked well and used sensibly it is extremely versatile. Here it is used with two of its root cousins – the humble carrot and the sweet potato – to create a delicious soup that is both nourishing and tasty.

1   Preheat the oven to 140°C/275°F/Gas Mark 1.

2   Place all of the vegetables along with the garlic and chilli in a baking tray. Sprinkle over the olive oil and salt and rub well to cover. Bake for 30–35 minutes, or until completely soft and cooked.

3   Transfer all the cooked vegetables to a casserole dish. Pour 500ml (18fl oz) or so of the boiling water into the baking tray and scrape and clean the vegetable remnants from the tray into the casserole dish. Add another 500ml (18fl oz) boiling water to the dish and set aside.

4   Heat the butter in a frying pan over a medium heat and add the cinnamon stick, cumin seeds and bay leaves. Sauté for a minute or so and add the ginger, curry leaves and coriander stalks and continue to sauté for a further minute or two.

5   Add these to the casserole dish of vegetables and place over a medium heat. Bring to a gradual boil. Simmer for 8–10 minutes and then remove and discard the cinnamon stick and bay leaves.

6   Let cool slightly and blitz to a purée. If the soup is too thick, add a little more boiling water to loosen.

7   Pass through a sieve if you would like a completely smooth texture, then return to the casserole dish and heat through. Check the seasoning and serve topped with some coriander.

Serves 6

Beetroot 2–3, trimmed and cut into small pieces
Carrots 2–3, trimmed and cut into small pieces
Sweet potato 1 small, cut into small pieces
Onion 1, quartered
Garlic 4–5 cloves, halved
Fresh green chillies 1–2, sliced
Olive oil 2 teaspoons
Sea salt 2 teaspoons
Boiling water 1 litre (1¾ pints)
Butter 2 tablespoons
Cinnamon stick 5cm (2in) piece
Cumin seeds 1½ teaspoons
Bay leaves 2–3
Fresh ginger 5–7.5cm (2–3in) piece, finely chopped
Curry leaves 12–15, preferably fresh, shredded; if using dried, soak in water for 10–12 minutes, and dry thoroughly before shredding
Fresh coriander 3–4 sprigs, leaves used for serving and the stalks for cooking

Tomato soup
Tamatar ka shorba

Tomato soup is perhaps the most popular soup in India and you will find it across the length and breadth of the country. Funnily enough, it is the British legacy that established it, with an Indian twist made here and there. I have gone semi-classical with my recipe and encourage you to tweak the flavours to make it your own. In my opinion, the croutons are a great addition.

1   Place the tomatoes in a casserole dish or saucepan, pour the stock or water over and bring to a boil over a medium–high heat.

2   Add the butter to a deep frying pan set over a medium heat and as soon as it melts, add the cumin, garlic and curry leaves. When the butter froths and the garlic changes colour ever so slightly, 1–2 minutes, add the rest of the vegetables and sauté until the onion is pale and soft, about 5–6 minutes. Add the flour and sauté for a few minutes until the roux has come together and is cooked through.

3   Add this roux to the tomatoes and simmer until all the vegetables are completely cooked through, around 10–12 minutes. Let cool slightly and blitz to a purée.

4   Return the soup to the dish or pan and reheat gently over a low heat while stirring often with a flat spatula. Do not place this over a high heat as the soup will stick to the bottom due to the flour content. Add some seasoning and serve with a drop of cream, some croutons or toasted chapatti pieces and some coriander or basil leaves, if you like.

Serves 4–5

Tomatoes 6–8 large, cut into pieces (use deep red ones such as beef tomatoes, but not plum)
Vegetable stock or water 1 litre (1¾ pints)
Butter or oil 3 tablespoons
Cumin seeds ½ teaspoon
Garlic 2–3 cloves, chopped
Curry leaves 10–12, preferably fresh, cut into pieces; if using dried, soak in water for 10–12 minutes, and dry thoroughly before cutting
Celery 1 stick, chopped
Carrot 1 small, sliced
Onion 1 medium, roughly chopped
Plain flour 2–3 tablespoons
Salt and freshly ground black pepper

To serve (optional)
Cream
Croutons or toasted chapatti
Coriander or basil leaves, chopped

4

SALADS

✳

Goat's cheese, roasted sweet potato & mixed leaf salad
Bakri kay doodh ka paneer, kaddu aur pattay ka salad

This hearty salad is delicious eaten anytime of the year. Try mixing in two or three different types of vegetarian goat's cheese – from the soft to the crumbly. The roasted sweet potato is a great match for the flavour of the goat's cheese and the prunes add extra sweetness, which will be cut through by the hot chilli dressing. You could also liven up a simple side salad with this dressing if you have some leftover.

1 Preheat the oven to 200°C/400°F/Gas Mark 6.

2 Place the red onion and sweet potato in a bowl and drizzle over the olive oil. Add some salt and pepper and mix together well. Arrange the onion skin-side down on a baking tray and spread the sweet potato alongside (do not wash the bowl just yet). Bake for roughly 20–30 minutes until both are cooked through, nicely coloured and crisp. Remove and let cool. Turn the oven down to 130°C/260°F/Gas Mark ¾.

3 Mix the nuts and seeds together and place on another baking tray. Cook for 10 minutes then switch off the oven and leave the tray inside.

4 To make the dressing, place the goat's cheese, lime juice, mustard, cumin seeds, green chilli, mint, coriander and olive oil in a bowl and mix well to form a paste. If needed, you can loosen the dressing with a little cream, a dash of milk or some more olive oil. Season to taste and set aside.

5 Peel and discard the onion skins and chop the onion and sweet potato into small pieces. Place in a large mixing bowl. Remove the nuts and seeds from the oven and, when completely cool, add half to the onion and sweet potato. Gently mix in the salad leaves, drizzle over the dressing and transfer to a serving bowl.

6 Sprinkle the prunes and remaining nuts and seeds over the top and serve with a sprinkling of ground cinnamon.

Serves 4–5

Red onion 1 large, unpeeled and cut into wedges
Sweet potato 1, cut into 1cm (½in) slices
Olive oil a drizzle
Raw skin-on almonds 3–4 tablespoons
Pine nuts 3–4 tablespoons
Sunflower seeds 1–2 tablespoons
Mixed baby salad leaves 1–2 handfuls
Sun-dried prunes 8–10, chopped
Ground cinnamon ½ teaspoon
Salt and freshly ground black pepper

For the dressing
Soft goat's cheese 120–130g (4–4½oz)
Lime juice from ½ lime
Hot English mustard 1 teaspoon
Cumin seeds ½ teaspoon, crushed
Fresh green chillies 1–2, chopped
Fresh mint 8–10 leaves, shredded
Fresh coriander 5–6 sprigs, leaves chopped
Olive oil 1 tablespoon
Cream, milk or olive oil (optional)

Note
The dressing can be made well in advance and kept in a small container. You can also make a smooth dressing by blitzing the ingredients in a blender to make a purée, which can be thinned down with a little water.

Cauliflower, beans, kale & walnut salad
Gobi, akhrot aur rajma salad

This is a great salad that is perfect for winter. I encourage you to create more combinations using any beans that you like – tinned or cooked – such as butter, red, flageolet, lima and black-eye. This salad is best served at room temperature or just warm as it gives the flavours in the dish time to infuse. Pictured overleaf (left).

1   Preheat the oven to 130°C/260°F/Gas Mark ¾.

2   Cook the walnuts on a baking tray for 10 minutes, then let cool and cut into pieces.

3   Blanch the cauliflower florets in a pan of boiling salted water for 4–5 minutes, until cooked but still crunchy, then remove with a slotted spoon and refresh under cold water. In the same cooking water, blanch the broccoli for 1–1½ minutes, and again remove and refresh. Add the kale to the boiling water, blanch for 3–4 minutes and refresh under cold water.

4   Drain the now cool vegetables, gently squeezing the cauliflower and broccoli and putting into a large serving bowl. Squeeze the kale leaves thoroughly to get rid of any excess water, then add to the bowl.

5   Refresh the beans quickly under some running water and add to the salad with the gherkin, spring onion and coriander.

6   To make the dressing, whisk together the mustard, garlic and vinegar with the cumin seeds and some salt and pepper. While still whisking, add the oil until it is smooth and creamy.

7   Just before serving, stir the dressing to combine and pour over the salad. Toss the salad together, sprinkle with the chopped walnuts and serve.

Serves 4–6

Walnuts 15–20, cut into pieces
Cauliflower 1, cut into small florets (save
   the stalks for another recipe)
Broccoli florets from a few stalks (save the
   stalks and stems for another recipe)
Curly kale 100–150g (3½–5½oz), chopped
Beans (see above) 1 x 400g (14oz) tin, drained
Gherkin 1, chopped (or pickled cucumber,
   capers or mini cornichons)
Spring onions 2–3, chopped
Fresh coriander 8–10 sprigs, leaves
   roughly chopped

For the dressing
Hot English mustard 1 tablespoon
Garlic 1 clove, crushed
White wine or cider vinegar 1 tablespoon
Cumin seeds 1 teaspoon, toasted and crushed
Extra-virgin rapeseed or olive oil
   2–3 tablespoons
Salt and freshly ground black pepper

Note
Use the drained water from the tin of beans for cooking – drain the liquid into some vegetable stock and use later to make soup.

Rice & bean salad
Chaawul aur kathor salad

The first thing to bear in mind when using leftover rice is health and safety. Once cooked, rice is one of the most dangerous foods in the house and we must be careful when using it. All freshly cooked rice should be decanted into a container with a well-fitting lid, but not shut straight away. Once at room temperature, place the rice open in the fridge until completely cooled down. Stir it once or twice and check if it is cold, then cover and store for a few days. If reheating, make sure it is piping hot all the way through. Pictured overleaf (right).

1   Refresh the chickpeas and sweetcorn under running water.

2   In boiling salted water, blanch the peas for 3 minutes, then refresh under cold water. Blanch the beans in the same water for 1 minute and refresh under cold water.

3   Place the rice, vegetables and spring onion in a bowl. Add the green chillies, coriander or parsley, but do not mix.

4   To make the dressing, toast the coriander and fennel seeds in a small dry frying pan over a medium heat for a minute until well scented. Let cool and then crush in a mortar.

5   Pour the olive oil and the balsamic into a small bowl, give it a stir, then add the crushed seeds and the garlic. Shred the basil, mint and dill leaves with a sharp knife, add to the dressing with the cumin seeds and mix together. Season.

6   When ready to serve, mix the dressing into the rice and vegetables and serve with the cheese sprinkled over the top.

Serves 4–5

Tinned chickpeas 120g (4oz)
Tinned sweetcorn 120g (4oz)
Green peas 120g (4oz), fresh or frozen
Beans 120g (4oz) **(any in season: broad beans, runners, borlotti, green or French)**
Leftover cooked rice 300g (10½oz) (arborio, basmati or wholegrain)
Spring onions 2 thin, finely sliced
Fresh green chillies 2 finger-type, deseeded and finely chopped
Fresh coriander or parsley ½ bunch, chopped

For the dressing
Coriander seeds 1 teaspoon
Fennel seeds ½ teaspoon
Extra-virgin olive or rapeseed oil 4–5 tablespoons
Balsamic vinegar ½ tablespoon
Garlic 1 clove, crushed
Fresh basil 20–25 leaves
Fresh mint 12–15 leaves
Fresh dill leaves from a few stalks, finely chopped
Cumin seeds ½ teaspoon, finely crushed
Cheddar 150g (5½oz), grated
Salt and freshly ground black pepper

> **Note**
> **Add pieces of boiled egg, potato and avocado, if you like.**

Yellow split peas, courgette, mint & olive salad
Channa daal, lauki aur olive ka salad

This may sound strange but this combination is actually delicious. All you need is some forward planning to get your ingredients together. For me, a salad needs to have some texture: it should be a little soft, have some crunch, have an immediate hit of flavour as well as a subtlety that will enhance the rest of your meal. Roasted seeds, nuts, pine nuts and toasted rice all make great additions to this.

1   Rinse the yellow split peas and soak in plenty of cold water for 3–4 hours. Once the split peas are well expanded and have absorbed water, drain and boil in a saucepan with a litre (1¾ pints) of water and the tomato pulp for 5–6 minutes or until just done. Drain, cool down and set aside.

2   Heat the oil in a wok or deep frying pan and add the mustard seeds. When they crackle, add the curry leaves, cumin seeds and garlic. After 2–3 minutes, when the garlic changes colour slightly, turn the heat down a little. Add the sesame seeds and peanuts and fry, stirring often to prevent burning, until both change colour to a pale brown, about 2–3 minutes.

3   As soon as the peanuts and sesame change colour, add the drained yellow split peas and sauté, stirring well until the split peas are nearly dry, about 10 minutes. Take off the heat and set aside to cool.

4   Preheat the oven to 200°C/400°F/Gas Mark 6.

5   Place the diced courgette in a bowl with the red chilli powder and combine with the teaspoon of oil. Roast the courgette for 6–8 minutes or until slightly caramelized, then remove and set aside to cool.

6   Place the remaining ingredients in a large serving dish with the lentils and mix well just before serving. Check the seasoning and add more oil before serving, if needed.

Serves 4–6

Yellow split peas (channa daal) 100–150g (3½–5½oz)
Plum or other firm tomatoes 2, pulp kept separate and flesh diced
Oil 2 tablespoons, plus 1 teaspoon for the courgettes
Black mustard seeds 1 teaspoon
Curry leaves 15–20, preferably fresh, shredded; if using dried, soak in water for 10–12 minutes, and dry thoroughly before shredding
Cumin seeds 1 teaspoon
Garlic 2–3 cloves, chopped
Sesame seeds 2 heaped tablespoons
Peanuts 2 heaped tablespoons
Courgettes 2, diced into 1cm (½in) pieces
Red chilli powder ½ teaspoon
Mixed pitted olives 80–100g (3–3½oz), halved or quartered
Cos or little gem lettuce 1 small, roughly chopped
Fresh mint 15–20 leaves, torn
Fresh coriander 4–5 sprigs, stalks and leaves chopped
Lime juice from ½ lime
Sea salt 1 teaspoon
Freshly ground black pepper ½ teaspoon

Note
You could add diced vegetarian feta cheese, boiled eggs or diced blanched beans. Mustard, roasted almonds and pine nuts are also good additions.

Fresh fennel & red onion salad with raw green mango
Taja sauf, laal pyaaz aur aam ka salaad

This is a very simple salad that I find works extremely well with grilled and barbecued foods, as well as in wraps and sandwiches. This recipe is very flexible and will work with whatever you have to hand, for example diced apple, avocado slices or you can even throw in some olives.

1   Mix together all of the dressing ingredients.

2   Gently toss the ingredients for the salad in a serving bowl and drizzle over the dressing. Top with the dill fronds when you are ready to serve.

Serves 5–6

Fennel 1 small, thoroughly washed and very thinly sliced
Red onions 2, very thinly sliced
Fresh mint 5–6 sprigs, leaves finely shredded
Chopped fresh coriander 2 tablespoons
Green chillies 2, finely chopped
Tomatoes 2, quartered and sliced or diced
Raw green mango ½, not too soft, peeled and chopped (**or use another type of mango**)
Dill fronds, to serve

For the dressing
Lime juice from 1 lime
Cider vinegar 2 teaspoons
Red chilli powder ½ teaspoon
Freshly ground black pepper ½ teaspoon
Olive oil 2–3 tablespoons
Salt ½ teaspoon

Broccoli, spinach, egg, toasted nuts & green bean salad

This is a salad that can easily be varied according to the ingredients available. And you can prep ahead: the nuts can be roasted ready for blending, the broccoli and beans can be blanched and chilled, and the eggs can be boiled and cooled. Pictured overleaf (left).

1   Blanch the broccoli in a pan of boiling salted water for 1–1½ minutes, then remove with a slotted spoon and refresh under cold water. In the same cooking water, blanch the beans for a minute at most, and again remove and refresh.

2   Preheat the oven to 120°C/250°F/Gas Mark ½.

3   Place the nuts on a small baking tray and cook for 15–20 minutes, then let cool and chop into pieces.

4   Boil the eggs for 7 minutes, turn off the heat and let them rest for a minute in the hot water. Drain and place in iced water to cool quickly. Peel and cut into pieces.

5   Increase the oven temperature to 150°C/300°F/Gas Mark 2. Mix together the ingredients for the seasoning and place on a baking tray lined with a silicon mat or baking parchment. Bake for 5 minutes. Remove from the oven, stir with a wooden spatula, then return to the oven. Keep repeating this process every 2 minutes until the sugar has melted into the other ingredients. When the sugar has melted, mix well and do not return the tray to the oven. Set aside to cool – it will form a crisp and crunchy seasoning.

6   In a small bowl, whisk together the mustard, lime juice and pepper. In a small pan, heat the olive oil to just below smoking and add the black mustard seeds. As soon as they start to crackle, pour the oil over the rest of the dressing ingredients. Season and mix well.

7   When ready to serve, place the beans, broccoli and spinach in a serving bowl and stir together.

8   Drizzle over some of the dressing and top with the toasted nuts and pieces of egg. Sprinkle over the seasoning, add a little more dressing and serve.

Serves 4–5

Broccoli ½ head, florets cut into small pieces
Green beans 1 handful, topped and tailed, cut into 1cm (½in) pieces
Cashew nuts, unskinned almonds and walnuts 1–2 tablespoons of each
Eggs 3–4
Fresh spinach 100g (3½oz) leaves, shredded, washed and drained
Chopped fresh coriander, to serve (optional)

For the dressing
English mustard 1 heaped teaspoon
Lime juice 1 tablespoon
Freshly ground black pepper
Extra-virgin olive oil 2–3 tablespoons
Black mustard seeds ½ teaspoon

For the seasoning
Fresh red chilli 1 tablespoon, crushed
White sugar 2 tablespoons
Sea salt 1 tablespoon
Cumin seeds 1½ teaspoons, crushed

Twisted Portuguese-style potato, black beans, vegetable & egg salad
Salada de batata e legumes com ovos e feijao preto

This salad is delicious served on its own or with a good chunk of warm bread.
Pictured overleaf (right).

1   Preheat the oven to 150°C/300°F/Gas Mark 2.

2   Place the potatoes in a roasting tray, drizzle over a small amount of oil and roast for 25–30 minutes. Remove from the oven, let cool and cut into eighths. Set aside.

3   Boil the eggs for 7½–8 minutes, then place in iced water to cool. When cold, peel and cut into eighths.

4   Blanch the beans in a pan of boiling salted water for 1 minute, then remove with a slotted spoon and refresh under cold water.

5   Heat the oil in a frying pan over a medium heat until just below smoking. Fry the mustard seeds, cumin seeds and green chilli. When the mustard seeds begin to crackle and splutter, add the green and black beans, toss, then switch off the heat and let cool. Once completely cooled, mix with all the remaining salad ingredients.

6   To make the dressing, whisk the vinegar with the olive oil and season to taste.

7   Drizzle the dressing over the salad and serve.

Serves 4–5

Baby potatoes 300–400g (10½–14oz)
Olive oil 1 tablespoon, plus extra for the potatoes
Eggs 3
Thin green beans 15–20, cut into 1cm (½in) pieces
Black mustard seeds ½ teaspoon
Cumin seeds 1 teaspoon
Fresh green chillies 1–2, finely chopped
Black beans 1 x 210g (7½oz) tin, drained and gently rinsed under cold water
Tomatoes 2–3, cut into pieces
Onion 1, roughly chopped
Red pepper 1, diced
Pitted black olives 20–25, whole or halved
Cucumber 1 small, diced
Fresh mint 10–15 leaves, chopped
Fresh coriander a few sprigs, chopped

For the dressing
Red wine vinegar 2 teaspoons
Extra-virgin olive oil 3–4 tablespoons
Salt and freshly ground black pepper

5

EASY
LUNCHES
- & -
SNACKS

*

Kale, potato, paneer & yellow split pea pakoras
Ghungaralee gobhi aloo paneer aur channa pakora

Pakoras, very simply, are pieces of meat, fish or vegetables dipped in any batter and fried. However, a pakora can also be a fritter, not dipped in batter, and with a combination of ingredients. For example, the most famous of all Indian snacks has got to be the onion 'bhujjia' (spelt 'bhajia' and misspelt 'bhaji'), which in the North of India would be called a pakora, though the word bhujjia would be clearly understood. Serve these with a fresh chutney or a dip as a snack or as part of a meal.

1 Soak the yellow split peas in plenty of cold water for 5–6 hours, or preferably overnight. Once soft, drain and crush or coarsely chop.

2 Boil the potato in a small pan of salted boiling water for 15 minutes, or until cooked and soft. Let cool, then peel and roughly crush.

3 In a large bowl, mix together all of the ingredients, except for the oil. Using a fork or potato masher, crush all the ingredients until combined.

4 Heat 2.5cm (1in) of oil in a deep frying pan over a medium heat. Drop a small dollop of the mixture in the hot oil; it should sizzle and stay whole. If the dollop breaks up in the oil, add a little more chickpea flour.

5 Take small handfuls of the mixture and form into small balls. In batches, deep-fry the balls until a deep golden brown and cooked through, about 4–5 minutes. Serve with a green chutney.

Makes 30–40 small pakoras

Yellow split peas (channa daal) 200g (7oz) (or any split peas: skinned and not whole)
Floury potato 1 large
Paneer 200g (7oz) (see page 190 for homemade), grated
Chickpea (gram) flour 4–5 heaped tablespoons
Fresh ginger 5–8cm (2–3in) piece, peeled and finely chopped
Garlic 2–3 cloves, finely chopped
Red onion 1, chopped
Fresh spinach leaves 1 handful, finely chopped
Kale or cavolo nero 1 large handful, finely chopped
Fresh mint 15–20 leaves, shredded
Chopped fresh coriander 1 heaped tablespoon
Ground cumin 1 teaspoon
Fresh green chillies 2–3 finger-type, finely chopped
Lime juice 1 tablespoon
Salt 1 teaspoon
Jeeravan masala (see page 189) 1 teaspoon
Oil for deep-frying
Salt and freshly ground black pepper

Spicy minced Indian paneer
Minced paneer kheema/bhurjee

A bhurjee is cooked with minced or finely chopped ingredients and is associated with items such as eggs, paneer and chicken. They are also very popular in North India, where paneer is cooked in squares or as a tikka – as the leftover paneer is used to make a bhurjee. A bhurjee goes very well with a pea pulao, can be added to rice or eaten with chapatti or naan. Or you can turn it into a wrap with a sweetish chutney, some sliced red onion, slivers of tomato, a few coriander and mint leaves and some thinly sliced peppers. Pictured overleaf (left).

1   Heat the oil in a casserole dish over a medium heat and add the garlic, ginger and chilli. When the garlic begins to colour after about 2 minutes, add the cumin. Sauté for a minute or two, then add the onion.

2   After the onion has softened, about 4–5 minutes, add the turmeric and chilli powders, increase the heat to high and add the tomatoes. While stirring, to ensure that nothing sticks to the bottom of the pan, sauté for a further 3–4 minutes until the tomato juices dry up. Lower the heat to medium and gently fold in the paneer.

3   Cook for 5 minutes or until the paneer is heated through and the pan is dry. Mix in the coriander, sprinkle over the jeeravan masala and serve with lime wedges.

Serves 4

Oil 2 tablespoons
Chopped garlic 1 tablespoon
Chopped fresh ginger
    1 tablespoon
Fresh green chillies 1–2 finger-
    type, chopped
Cumin seeds 1 heaped teaspoon,
    crushed
Onions 2, finely chopped
Ground turmeric ½ teaspoon
Red chilli powder 1 teaspoon
Tomatoes 2, pulp removed and
    flesh chopped
Paneer 400g (14oz) (see page 190
    for homemade), finely chopped
    (or halloumi or grated
    mozzarella)
Chopped fresh coriander
    1½ heaped tablespoons
Jeeravan masala (see page 189)
    ½ teaspoon (optional)
Lime 1, to serve

Aunty Freny's green bean cutlets
Freny aunty na fansi na cutless

The Freny Aunty I am referring to is my mother-in-law Freny, and this is one of her favourite dishes. All of her children grew up on these and so did our kids, who still love them. The dish is nothing but potato and chopped French beans, rolled in breadcrumbs or semolina and fried. This recipe is a slight variation and hopefully my mother-in-law won't mind. Eat these with a tomato sauce or dip, as part of a larger meal or in a bun like a burger. Pictured overleaf (right).

1   Peel the potatoes, cut into thick slices and boil in salted water until cooked, about 5–7 minutes. Drain, return to the same pan and, with a flat wooden spatula, dry the slices out over a low flame until any moisture has been dried out and the potatoes are semi-mashed. Mash with a fork or masher and transfer to a small tray to let cool.

2   Heat a tablespoon of oil in a frying pan over a medium heat and add the green chilli, ginger and garlic. As soon as the garlic changes colour, about 2 minutes, add the onion and continue cooking for about 5 minutes until soft. Keep an eye on the pan and if the contents start to stick, add a little water.

3   Meanwhile, mix the cumin, coriander and turmeric with a little water to form a paste. Add the paste to the cooked onion, adding more water to the bowl to remove any powder stuck to it and adding this to the pan too. Cook until the liquid is all evaporated.

4   Mix in the cooled potato and season well. Split into 6–8 equal-sized portions and form into balls. Dust the palms of your hands with a bit of flour and flatten one of the balls. Place a portion of the blanched (and completely dry) beans in the centre and carefully fold the potato over to cover.

5   Place on your work surface and shape into a patty, making sure the beans are well enclosed. Roll them in the semolina and set aside. Repeat with all the remaining mixture.

6   Heat the oil in a large frying pan over a medium heat. Shallow-fry the patties in batches, cooking for 3–4 minutes on each side or until both sides are golden brown and crisp. Remove from the oil and place on a plate lined with some kitchen paper to absorb any excess oil. Serve hot with chilli ketchup, a fresh chutney or any sauce of your choice.

Serves 6–8

Potatoes 2–3 large
Oil 200ml (7fl oz) plus 1 tablespoon
Fresh green chillies 2, finely chopped
Fresh ginger 5cm (2in) piece, peeled and finely chopped
Garlic 2 cloves, chopped
Onion 1, chopped
Ground cumin ½ teaspoon
Ground coriander ¾ teaspoon
Ground turmeric ¼ teaspoon
Plain flour, for dusting
Green beans 250–300g (9–10½oz), blanched (see page 23), thoroughly dried and chopped
Semolina 4–5 tablespoons
Salt

Note
For extra flavour, you can add crushed toasted cumin seeds to the mashed potato just before forming it into balls.
   You can make these in advance and keep on some kitchen paper. Just reheat in a hot oven. They will keep very well for 2–3 days.

Red cabbage & kale bhajee
Laal bundh gobi aur karam saag ki bhaji

This is a very simple dish to prepare and is especially great when both the vegetables are in season. Red cabbage is generally quite tightly packed and dense, which can make it difficult to slice. Use a lighter one if you can find it as it will allow you to shred the leaves a little thinner and finer, but don't worry if not.

1   Place a wok or a kadhai over a medium–high heat, add the oil and heat until hot but not yet smoking.

2   Add the cumin seeds and as soon as they change colour, add the ginger and garlic and green chilli. Sauté until the garlic changes colour, about 2–3 minutes, then add the onion and cook for 5–6 minutes or until soft and pale.

3   Add the cabbage and kale and mix them in well. Sauté for around 10 minutes, stirring often, cooking until the cabbage and kale are cooked but still crunchy. Add the lime juice and cook for a few more seconds. Add a little seasoning and serve.

Serves 4–6 as a side

Oil 3 tablespoons
Cumin seeds 1 tablespoon
Fresh ginger 5cm (2in) piece, peeled and finely chopped
Garlic 2 cloves, finely crushed
Fresh green chillies 1–2 finger-type, thinly sliced
Red onions 2 small, thinly sliced
Red cabbage ⅓, core removed, sliced very thinly
Kale 10–12 leaves, tough central stalk removed, leaves thinly sliced
Lime juice from ½ lime
Salt

Bread & potato sandwich pakora
Aloo aur dubbel roti ka pakora

While this pakora is sometimes eaten for breakfast and found at motorway lay-bys in India, it is more often enjoyed as a mid-afternoon snack or a late-morning brunch. Serve with a fresh green chutney, hot sauce or ketchup. These are great for a party, where they can be cut into smaller pieces and served as a canapé. But the best way to eat these is on a cool day with a hot cup of ginger and cardamom chai.

1   Place all of the ingredients for the filling in a bowl and mix together well. Season to taste, then set aside.

2   To make the batter, sift the chickpea flour into a bowl. Add all the remaining ingredients except the oil for frying and beat together to form a smooth batter the consistency of single cream. Add a bit more water if needed. Set aside for a few minutes, but don't make the batter too far in advance.

3   Lay half the bread slices on the worktop and divide the filling evenly between them. Spread the filling to cover the slices completely, then top with the remaining slices and flatten so tightly sealed. Cut into whatever shape you prefer: triangles, rectangles or smaller squares.

4   Place a deep frying pan over a medium–high heat and add roughly 1cm (½in) of oil.

5   Dip each sandwich piece into the batter so that it is completely covered, then very carefully add it to the hot oil, being careful not to splash any of the hot oil.

6   Fry until nice and golden on both sides, then place in a colander to drain. Transfer to a plate lined with kitchen paper to absorb any excess oil. Serve hot.

Makes 6–8

For the filling
Potatoes 2 large, boiled, cooled, peeled and grated
Red chilli powder ½ teaspoon
Cumin seeds ¾ teaspoon, toasted and crushed
Fresh green chillies 2–3 finger-type, finely chopped
Chopped fresh mint leaves 1 tablespoon
Chopped fresh coriander 2 tablespoons
Lime juice a drizzle
Salt

For the batter
Chickpea (gram) flour 250–300g (9–10½oz)
Red chilli powder ½ teaspoon
Garam masala (see page 186) ¼ teaspoon (optional)
Cumin seeds ½ teaspoon, toasted and crushed
Coriander seeds ½ teaspoon, toasted and crushed
Asafoetida a good pinch (optional)
Bicarbonate of soda a good pinch
Water 150ml (5fl oz)
Oil 1 teaspoon, plus extra for frying
White bread 6–8 slices

Marrow & potato kofta
Dudhee aloo kofta

These koftas are great as a canapé or snack – simply serve them with a spiced yogurt dip or a mayonnaise-based sauce. They are also great when immersed in the tomato sauce on page 192 and served as a main meal with rice and bread.

1   Line a sieve with a muslin or clean tea towel. Place the grated marrow in a saucepan and cover with some water. Add a little salt and bring to the boil for 1–2 minutes. Drain in the colander and squeeze out any excess water. Place in a mixing bowl, fluff with a fork and let cool.

2   Scoop out the flesh of the potato and mash, then mix into the marrow. Stir in the chickpea flour, chilli, ginger, pepper and some salt until well combined.

3   Equally divide the mixture into 12–14 golf-ball-sized balls.

4   Stir together the prunes and almonds and equally divide into as many balls as the marrow mixture.

5   Wet your hands a little and flatten each marrow ball. Place a ball of the prune mixture into the middle of each. Close the marrow mixture over the stuffing to form a ball once again.

6   Refrigerate for at least 30 minutes to let them firm.

7   Once firm, heat 1cm (½in) of oil in a deep pan or wok over a medium heat and roll the koftas in a little extra flour.

8   Carefully place one kofta in the oil to check that it does not split or break. If they do crack, roll them again in a little more flour.

9   Fry the koftas a few at a time for 5–8 minutes, turning frequently until well coloured on all sides. Remove from the oil and drain well on some kitchen paper. Let the oil reheat before frying the next batch.

Makes 12–14 koftas

Marrow 1 large, peeled, deseeded and grated
Potatoes 2 medium, baked in their skins until soft
Chickpea (gram) flour 120g (4oz), plus extra for rolling
Fresh green chillies 2, deseeded and very finely chopped
Finely chopped fresh ginger 1 heaped tablespoon
Freshly ground black pepper ½ teaspoon
Prunes 16–18, chopped into small pieces
Almonds 20, roughly chopped
Oil for frying
Salt
Yogurt or yogurt and mint sauce (page 177) to serve

Baked spicy falafels
Cholay kay bhajjiyay

Simple, nutritious and easy to make for a great pre-dinner or afternoon snack or as part of a meal. I call them falafel as it is the most recognized term when it comes to chickpea cakes. In India, chickpeas are really big and in the Punjab they are very much a staple.

1 Rinse the chickpeas, then soak in water that covers them by 2–3cm (1in) for a minimum of 4 hours. The longer the better, but after a few hours, place in the fridge to continue soaking or they will start to ferment.

2 Preheat the oven to 150°C/300°F/Gas Mark 2.

3 Pour the 2 tablespoons of olive oil onto a large baking tray and spread out to evenly coat the tray.

4 Drain the chickpeas and refresh in some cold water. Place them in a food processor with the garlic, onion, chillies, ginger, coriander and cumin seeds, fresh coriander, salt, some pepper and the 2–3 tablespoons of olive oil. Blitz for about 1 minute until smooth.

5 Scoop out about 2 tablespoons of the mixture at a time. Shape the falafel mixture into small patties, about 5cm (2in) wide and 1cm (½in) thick. Place each falafel onto the oiled tray.

6 Bake for 25–30 minutes, carefully flipping the falafels halfway through baking, until they are golden brown on both sides.

7 Place the falafels in a pita or on a bed of greens and drizzle with the tahini to serve.

Serves 4–6

Dried chickpeas 250–300g (9–10½oz)
Olive oil 2–3 tablespoons, plus 2 tablespoons for greasing
Garlic 4–5 cloves
Red onion 1, roughly chopped
Fresh green chillies 3–4 finger-type
Fresh ginger 5cm (2in) piece, peeled and roughly chopped
Coriander seeds 2 teaspoons, toasted and finely crushed
Cumin seeds 1 teaspoon, toasted and roughly crushed
Chopped fresh coriander 2 tablespoons
Sea salt 1 heaped teaspoon
Freshly ground black pepper
Tahini, to serve

Raymond & Mandy Lockwood's cauliflower rice
Gobhi ka kheema

The Lockwoods have been Café Spice Namasté well-wishers and regular customers for some time now. In recent years, the words 'diet-and-low-carb' have come onto the scene and a request for cauliflower 'rice' emerged. We prefer to call it 'kheema' as it is very popular in India and can be made using several vegetables, for example cauliflower, broccoli, cabbage, carrot and sweetcorn. You can even use a combination of leftover vegetables to create a very unique dish.

1   Separate the stalk and stems from the cauliflower and set the florets aside. Carefully wash the stalks and stems, drain and blitz them in a food processor, or very finely chop them with a knife. Repeat this process with the florets and keep separate.

2   Toast the cumin and coriander seeds in a small dry frying pan over a medium heat until aromatic, about 30 seconds. When cooled, crush them in a mortar to the consistency of crushed peppercorns.

3   Place the cauliflower stalks and stems in a large frying pan, spread out evenly with a spatula and add just enough water to cover. Cover the pan and cook for 5–6 minutes. Add the florets and the butter, cover again and cook for another 3–4 minutes, then drain in a sieve set over a bowl to collect the liquid.

4   Wipe out the pan with a piece of kitchen paper, set over a medium heat and add the oil. When hot, add the ginger and garlic and sauté until the garlic changes colour slightly, about 2 minutes, then add the crushed cumin and coriander. Sauté for a few seconds and then add the onion and green chilli.

5   When the onion turns pale and soft, about 5 minutes, add the turmeric. A few seconds later, add the tomato and any liquid collected from the strained cauliflower. Cook for 5–6 minutes, until the liquid dries out a little, then cook the pepper for a minute and add the cauliflower.

6   Drizzle with lime juice and season. Heat everything through until the mixture is almost dry. Serve with some slices of fresh green chilli sprinkled on top.

Serves 4–5 as a side

Cauliflower 500g (1lb 2oz)
Cumin seeds 1 teaspoon
Coriander seeds 1 heaped
    teaspoon
Butter 1 tablespoon
Oil 2 tablespoons
Fresh ginger 5cm (2in) piece,
    peeled and finely chopped
Garlic 4 cloves, finely chopped
Onions 2 medium, chopped
Fresh green chillies 2 finger-type,
    slit into 4 lengthways plus extra
    to serve
Ground turmeric ½ teaspoon
Tomato 1, chopped
Green pepper 1 small, chopped
Lime juice 1 teaspoon
Salt

Note
This can be stirred into rice or pasta, which will add variety and flavour. You can also add tiny cubes of fried aubergine.

Pascal's butternut squash hummus

A friend of ours in France grows so many butternut squashes each year that his poor wife got sick of seeing them, let alone eating them. We received so many emails asking what else they could do with them. So here is a simple recipe that resembles a hummus, but has the added flavour of roast butternut squash. This idea came from Vancouver, where our professor friend is always experimenting. Eat with toasted pita bread strips or simply lap it up.

1   Preheat the oven to 200°C/400°F/Gas Mark 6.

2   Place all the ingredients, except for the chickpeas, tahini and cumin seeds, in a bowl and toss until well mixed. Transfer to a baking tray and pour the liquid from the tin of chickpeas into the tray (but not the chickpeas themselves).

3   Roast for 20 minutes to give the butternut squash some colour, then cover loosely with foil and roast for another 25 minutes until the squash is fully cooked and soft. Remove and set aside to cool.

4   Peel the garlic or squeeze out the pulp from each clove and add to a food processor with the rest of the ingredients in the baking tray. Add the remaining olive oil, the chickpeas, tahini and cumin seeds and blitz to a smooth, thick paste.

5   Scrape the hummus into a bowl. Before serving, drizzle over some red chilli oil or a good pesto, if you like.

Serves 6–8 as a dip

Butternut squash ½ small (400g/14oz), peeled and roughly chopped
Garlic 4–5 cloves, unpeeled
Green chillies 2, split in half lengthways
Green pepper 1, quartered
Red pepper 1, quartered
Olive oil 2 tablespoons, plus 2 tablespoons for blending
Chickpeas 1 x 400g (14oz) tin
Tahini 3–4 tablespoons
Cumin seeds 1 teaspoon, toasted
Salt and freshly ground black pepper
Red chilli oil or pesto to serve (optional)

Split pea fritters
The Sun-Seeker channa daal aloo wada

Aloo wada, or bonda as they are often called, are table-tennis-sized or larger fritters of crushed, spiced potato dipped in chickpea batter and fried. They are served as a snack or as a meal, stuffed in soft bread rolls or as an accompaniment to other foods. I gave this name to these wadas as I was doing a class for the Sun-Seeker folks and was not given all the right ingredients. However, I was saved when I found split yellow peas in a little bag tucked away in the larder and two large jacket potatoes in the fridge. Serve with fresh green chutney or tamarind and date sauce.

1   Soak the yellow split peas in cold water for 3–4 hours or overnight.

2   Boil the potatoes in salted boiling water for 10–15 minutes until cooked and soft. Peel and crush with a potato masher until no lumps remain. Spread the potato out on a tray and set aside.

3   Drain the yellow split peas and check that they break easily and almost crumble if squeezed or rubbed between your fingers.

4   Heat the 2 tablespoons of oil in a casserole dish over a medium heat until a haze forms on top. Drop in a couple of mustard seeds – the oil is hot enough when a little foam forms around the seeds and they start to crackle. Add the mustard seeds and let them crackle, keeping the pot slightly covered as it keeps the seeds from spluttering. After about 10–15 seconds, add the cumin, ginger, curry leaves and the green chilli. Sauté for a few seconds, then add the yellow split peas.

5   Sauté for a minute or two, stirring well to prevent the peas from sticking to the bottom of the dish, and then add the onion. As less oil is used, the onion will stick, so keep stirring until the onion becomes pale, about 5–6 minutes.

6   Add the turmeric and continue to cook for a minute or so, then pour the mixture over the crushed potato, scraping anything stuck to the bottom of the pan. Mix in well, season and stir in the coriander.

7   Push the mixture towards one side of the tray and divide into equal portions, to the size you wish to make. If you want to prepare them for snacks, then you probably need small 2.5cm (1in) bondas, but if you wish to eat them like veggie burgers, as they do in Bombay, then you will need to make them fairly large. While you make the batter, place the bondas in a sieve set over a bowl so that they can drain.

Makes 12–15 fritters

Yellow split peas (channa daal) 100g (3½oz)
Potatoes 2 large
Oil 2 tablespoons, plus extra for frying
Black mustard seeds 1 teaspoon
Cumin seeds 1 teaspoon
Finely chopped fresh ginger 2 teaspoons
Fresh curry leaves 12, preferably fresh, finely shredded; if using dried, soak in water for 10–12 minutes, and dry thoroughly before shredding
Fresh green chillies 2 finger-type, very finely chopped
Onion 1, chopped
Ground turmeric 1 teaspoon
Chopped fresh coriander 1 heaped tablespoon
Chickpea (gram) flour 150g (5½oz)
Oil for deep-frying
Salt

Continued overleaf

8   Sift the flour into a bowl. Slowly pour cold water into the flour, whisking all the time. The batter needs to be liquid enough to pour and the consistency of double cream.

9   Heat a deep pan filled with 5–7.5cm (2–3in) of oil over a medium heat. The oil is ready when a little bit of the batter is dropped into it and it pops straight up instead of sitting at the bottom. Dip each potato ball into the batter and allow any excess batter to drip from the ball. Watching all the time, fry until they slightly change colour, but not until they brown. If you do let them brown, then the batter will be overcooked. They should look quite firm. Serve hot.

Note
Instead of using yellow split peas, replace them with any other split pea available, or alternatively you can use fava beans or marrow peas.
   For even more flavour, add some fresh shredded spinach.

Saffron sticky rice filled with mushrooms & cheese
Fofos de arroz com açafrão queijo e cogumelos

This is a brilliant twist on Italian arancini. The aromatic rice is delicious fried as little bite-sized balls. You can use a mix of different vegetarian cheeses, so use whatever you prefer – I have just suggested the combination that I normally use. Experiment and have fun with the recipe!

1   Cook the rice according to the packet instructions, then drain in a colander. While it is still hot, stir in the saffron until well mixed. Cover, set aside to cool, and once cool place the rice in the fridge to chill.

2   Meanwhile, get the filling ready. Heat the oil in a large frying pan over a medium heat and when the oil is smoking, add the mushrooms. Do not stir initially, but after a minute stir once, then let it rest again.

3   When the mushrooms are nearly dry, add the cumin seeds, spring onion and the green chilli and cook with the mushrooms until the spring onion is pale and dry, about 3–4 minutes. Season, add the coriander and turn off the heat.

4   Once the mushroom mixture has cooled, stir in the cheese and season.

5   Make 12 equal-sized balls of the rice and 12 equal-sized balls of the mushroom mixture. Using your hands, flatten each rice ball to roughly a 5mm (¼in) thickness. Place a ball of the mushroom mixture at the centre of the flattened rice and completely cover it with the rice to make a larger ball. Repeat with all of the mixture.

6   Dip each ball in the flour and dust off any excess, then dip into the beaten egg and finally roll in the breadcrumbs.

7   Heat the oil in a wok or a kadhai over a medium–high heat until very hot. Fry the balls for 1–2 minutes until golden brown all over and completely heated through.

Makes 12 balls

Jasmine, sticky or sushi rice 250g (9oz)
Saffron threads a pinch, crushed to a powder
Oil 2 teaspoons
Mixed mushrooms 200g (7oz), sliced or chopped
Cumin seeds 1 teaspoon
Spring onions 2, finely chopped
Fresh green chillies 2 finger-type, finely chopped
Chopped fresh coriander 1 heaped tablespoon
Cheese: I use a 5cm (2in) piece of strong Cheddar, a 5cm (2in) piece of blue and a 5cm (2in) piece of hard cheese, grated
Plain flour 100g (3½oz)
Eggs 2, beaten
Breadcrumbs, panko or semolina 200g (7oz)
Oil for frying
Salt and freshly ground black pepper

6

MAINS

✿

Baked tandoori-style cauliflower with giant couscous
Tandoori phool gobhi aur couscous

The cauliflower and couscous are delicious when eaten as separate dishes too.

1 Trim the cauliflower of all its leaves and cut off the stalk. Save these for making a soup.

2 Cut the cauliflower in half and then cut thick, roughly 1cm (½in) steak-like slices from each half. Add the salt and pepper and rest for a few minutes.

3 Mix together all the marinade ingredients.

4 Grease 2 baking trays or line them with baking parchment. Preheat the oven to 160°C/325°F/Gas Mark 3.

5 Rub the marinade onto the cauliflower slices and place on the prepared trays. Set aside for 10–15 minutes.

6 Boil the couscous in just enough water to cover for 10–12 minutes, then drain well.

7 Place the cauliflower in the oven. Bake for 15 minutes, then turn the slices over using tongs, and return to the oven for another 10 minutes or until cooked through and well coloured on both sides. Be sure to switch the tray height to ensure even colouring.

8 Meanwhile, heat the oil in a large frying pan over a medium heat and fry the cumin seeds and dried chilli until fragrant, then add the garlic and the green chilli. Add the butter and sauté the garlic until it is slightly coloured, about 2–3 minutes. Then add the spinach and sauté until wilted, another 4–5 minutes.

9 Stir in the boiled couscous and cook for a couple of minutes, until heated through. Season to taste and add the coriander.

10 Serve the cauliflower steaks hot, on top of the couscous.

Serves 4

Cauliflower 1 large
Salt 1 teaspoon
Freshly ground black pepper ½ teaspoon

For the marinade
Full-fat Greek-style yogurt 2 tablespoons
Oil 1 tablespoon
Red chilli powder 1 teaspoon
Ground turmeric ½ teaspoon
Ground coriander 1 teaspoon
Cumin seeds 1 teaspoon, well crushed
Tomato paste 2 teaspoons
English mustard 1 teaspoon
Lime juice from ½ lime
Finely crushed fresh ginger 2 teaspoons

For the couscous
Giant couscous 250g (9oz)
Oil 2 teaspoons
Cumin seeds 1 teaspoon
Dried red chillies 2–3, deseeded
Garlic 3–4 cloves, thinly sliced
Fresh green chillies 2–3, finely chopped
Butter 1 tablespoon
Fresh spinach 2 handfuls, roughly shredded
Chopped fresh coriander 1–2 heaped
 tablespoons
Salt and freshly ground black pepper

Note
You can add chopped tomatoes to the cooked spinach. Cook until soft but still wet, then stir through the couscous.
   When the couscous is cool, you can eat it as a salad. Just add sliced olives, vegetarian cheese (such as soft blue, brie or goat's cheese) or some shredded vegetables such as carrot or beetroot.

Mushrooms with paneer & peppers
Dhingri paneer ka dolma

This is a really simple recipe that is great as a weeknight dinner when you don't have too much time and you want a satisfying meal. Eat with some rice or bread or you can even pour this over some freshly cooked pasta.

1   Heat the oil in a wok or a kadhai over a medium heat and add the cardamom. As soon as the cardamom changes colour, add the cumin and fennel seeds and sauté for about 30 seconds, or until they start to colour.

2   Add the ginger & garlic paste and continue stirring and cooking until almost dry, about 2–3 minutes, then add the spring onion and red chilli powder. Sauté for a minute or so and add the tomatoes.

3   Sauté until the tomatoes mostly dry out, about 5–6 minutes, then add the mushrooms and increase the heat. As soon as the moisture evaporates, add the peppers and keep the heat on high. Sauté for a few seconds, then add the paneer, and ginger and green chillies and continue to sauté for about a minute or until the paneer is heated through.

4   Take off the heat, check the seasoning, mix in the chopped coriander and serve.

Serves 4–5

Extra-virgin rapeseed oil 3–4 tablespoons
Green cardamom pods 2, split
Cumin seeds 1 teaspoon
Fennel seeds ¼ teaspoon
Ginger & garlic paste (see page 188)
    2 tablespoons
Spring onions 4–5, chopped
Red chilli powder 1 teaspoon
Tomatoes 4, chopped
Button mushrooms 250–300g (9–10½oz),
    thickly sliced
Green pepper 1 small, sliced
Red pepper 1 small, sliced
Paneer 450g (1lb) (see page 190 for
    homemade), cut into 1cm (½in) cubes
Fresh ginger 5cm (2in) piece, peeled and
    very thinly sliced
Fresh green chillies 2 finger-type, slit into
    4 lengthways
Freshly ground black pepper ½ teaspoon
Chopped fresh coriander 1 tablespoon
Salt

Note
You can cook this in advance. Cook the mushrooms and tomato until semi-dry and when ready to serve, reheat the sauce and finish the dish as above.

Grandma Todiwala's macaroni & cauliflower cheese
Bapaiji Todiwala ni gobi nay macaroni cheese

This was Mum's all-time favourite dinner for us when we were kids. It goes back to when the first pasta was introduced to the British public and promptly found its way to India and into the clubs and gymkhanas of the Raj. Like most Indians, I grew up eating over-boiled pasta. It was not until my European training back in 1980 that I realized we had been cooking it all wrong – but in those days if you cooked pasta al dente it was sent back to you. Mum's macaroni was cooked until it split, but hey, the fun was in the sauce and her awesome magic with taste.

1   Bring the water to the boil in a pan. Add a little salt and boil the florets for 4–5 minutes at most. Remove with a slotted spoon, refresh under cold water in a bowl and drain.

2   To the same pan, add the macaroni and cook according to the packet instructions. Remove with a slotted spoon, refresh under cold water and drain. Mix with the cauliflower.

3   Add the cauliflower trimmings and stems to the water and cook for 5 minutes until very soft. Blitz the cauliflower and some of the water to a purée. You need to have about 250–300ml (8½–10fl oz).

4   Preheat the oven to 200°C/400°F/Gas Mark 6. Generously grease the inside of the baking dish with butter.

5   Melt the butter in a large saucepan and add the cumin seeds. Heat for 30 seconds, then take off the heat. Add the flour and stir in well. Whisk in the milk and some of the puréed cauliflower until well blended.

6   Return the saucepan to the heat and stir well but gently with the whisk. From time to time, scrape with a spatula to ensure it is not sticking to the bottom. Bring to the boil and simmer for a few minutes, adding more puréed cauliflower if needed, until it is the consistency of white sauce. Add the green chilli, chilli powder and some seasoning.

7   Stir half the cheese into the sauce and mix until the cheese has melted and the sauce is smooth. Take off the heat and add the mustard, macaroni and cauliflower to the sauce and mix well but gently. Add the coriander and check everything is well coated in sauce – if needed, add some more purée.

8   Transfer the mixture to the baking dish. Combine the remaining cheese with the breadcrumbs and sprinkle over the top. Bake for about 15–20 minutes until the topping is golden and crisp. Serve immediately.

Serves 4–5

Water 1 litre (1¾ pints)
Cauliflower florets 300g (10½oz), (reserve the stems and trimmings)
Dried macaroni 300g (10½oz)
Butter 2 heaped tablespoons, plus extra for greasing
Cumin seeds ½ teaspoon
Plain flour 4 tablespoons, sifted
Whole milk 400ml (14fl oz)
Fresh green chillies 2–3 finger-type, finely chopped
Red chilli powder a pinch
Cheddar 200–300g (7–10½oz), grated
Hot English mustard 3–4 teaspoons
Chopped fresh coriander 1 heaped tablespoon
Fresh breadcrumbs 3–4 tablespoons
Salt and freshly ground black pepper

Notes
You can also use green peas, potatoes, carrot or broccoli, but there is nothing quite like using just cauliflower for its unique taste and flavour.

Okra in tamarind sauce
Imli wali bhindi

Friend to some, enemy to others, the highly nutritious okra, aka bhindi, suffers from a great love-hate divide. Over the years I have been able to determine that for many, the hate comes from the fact that as a child you were probably forced to eat gloopy, sticky, gooey okra, prepared by a mother who was battling against time in order to feed a hungry family. However, okras are delicious, tasty and packed sky high with nutrients. Below is a simple recipe, where the acidity in the tamarind curtails the gloop that may emanate under normal cooking methods. Serve with daal and rice.

1   Heat a large frying pan over a medium heat until hot. Add 2 tablespoons of the oil and the okra. Do not stir too often as this will cool down the pan and release moisture. Toss after a minute or so and, once slightly browned, remove to a plate lined with kitchen paper.

2   Place the coriander, chilli powder and turmeric in a small bowl and make a thin paste with the water. Cover and set aside.

3   Heat the remaining oil in heavy-based saucepan or a casserole dish over a medium heat, add the onion and a pinch of salt and sauté for approximately 3–4 minutes or until the onion is pale. Add the garlic paste and continue to cook for roughly 2 minutes, or until the onion is light golden in colour.

4   Add the green chilli and sauté for 30 seconds, then mix well. Stir in the spice paste and cook for 2–3 minutes, or until all the moisture has evaporated and oil begins to appear at the edges.

5   Stir in the tomatoes and continue to cook for roughly 3–4 minutes, or until the oil appears and rises to the surface. Add the tamarind a little at a time (to taste) and cook for a minute or so.

6   Mix the sugar into a cup of water and pour into the pan. Season, bring the sauce to a gentle boil and then reduce to a simmer for 2–3 minutes.

7   Place a small frying pan over a medium heat; this will be used for the tempering. Add the oil and as soon as it starts to form a haze, add a couple of mustard seeds to check if it is hot enough. If the seeds crackle and form tiny bubbles around the edges, then the oil is ready. Keep a lid ready as the seeds will splutter.

Serves 4

Extra-virgin rapeseed oil 4–5 tablespoons

Okra 500g (1lb 2oz) washed, drained, dried thoroughly, trimmed and roughly chopped

Ground coriander 1 heaped tablespoon

Red chilli powder 1 heaped teaspoon

Ground turmeric ½ teaspoon

Water 100ml (3½fl oz)

Onions 2 small, finely chopped

Garlic 4 cloves, ground to a paste

Fresh green chillies 2 finger-type, slit into 4 and chopped

Tomatoes 250g (9oz), chopped

Light Thai tamarind paste 50ml (2fl oz)

Sugar 1 heaped teaspoon

Salt

8   Add the remaining mustard seeds along with the cumin seeds, and as soon as they start to splutter, lightly cover the pan. Reduce the heat to low, add the curry leaves and stir-fry for about a minute, or until they stop spluttering and are fragrant. Pour the oil and all of the spices into the sauce. Stir well and add the okra.

9   Let simmer for a minute or so, then switch off the heat and check the seasoning. Do not let the okra overcook. Top with some coriander, if you like, and serve.

For the tempering
Extra-virgin rapeseed oil
   1 tablespoon
Black mustard seeds ½ teaspoon
Cumin seeds 1 teaspoon
Curry leaves 10–15, preferably
   fresh, shredded; if using dried,
   soak in water for 10–12 minutes,
   and dry thoroughly before
   shredding
Fresh coriander, chopped, to serve
   (optional)

Note
Fennel seeds taste very good with a tomato-based sauce, so fry some fennel seeds along with the cumin.

Banana & thrice-cooked potato in yogurt
Dahi may kaela aur teen bar talay huay aloo

A simple preparation of pan-fried banana and potatoes, gently spiced and blended with yogurt. The frying and cooking of bananas or plantains is usually thought of as South Indian, but in several parts of India this practice is also common, and among us Parsees, fried, nicely caramelized plantains were a usual sight on the dining table with daal and rice. It was a cheaper option than putting meat on the table. Serve on its own with hot chapattis or parathas or as an accompaniment.

1   Place the potato cubes in salted boiling water for 6–8 minutes or until cooked. Drain and leave in the colander to allow them to dry out.

2   Heat the oil or ghee in a large frying pan over a medium heat. Do not overheat – heat just until you see a very light haze form on the surface. Cooking a few of the potatoes at a time, sauté until all the sides are nicely browned, about 3–4 minutes. Remove the cubes as they brown and place back in the colander, this time with a bowl underneath to collect any oil or ghee. Repeat the process with more of the cubes.

3   When they are all browned, wipe off any bits of potato sticking to the pan, pour the collected oil or ghee in the bowl back into it and reheat.

4   Once the pan is hot, repeat the process with the banana, letting the pieces caramelize well and flipping them over with a fork when one side is done. Keep an eye on them as they can quickly burn. Lift out of the pan and place on a plate lined with kitchen paper to let drain.

5   Reheat any oil or ghee left in the pan, add the asafoetida, if using, and cumin seeds and stir-fry for a minute or until the seeds splutter. Add the chilli powder, ginger and spring onion and sauté until pale, 1–2 minutes, then add the potato and banana and toss for a minute or two.

6   Gently mix the yogurt with the water and the ground cinnamon and pour over the potato mixture.

7   Mix well, add some seasoning and cover the pan. Let simmer for 3–4 minutes until the yogurt has broken down and everything is well cooked. Add the mint and coriander, mix well and serve.

Serves 4

Potatoes 4 large, peeled and cubed
Extra-virgin rapeseed oil or ghee 4–5 tablespoons
Bananas 4–5 or plantains 2 large, cut into 1cm (½in) slices
Asafoetida ¼ teaspoon (optional)
Cumin seeds 1 teaspoon
Red chilli powder ¾ teaspoon
Fresh ginger 5cm (2in) piece, peeled, finely chopped and crushed
Spring onions 2–3, thickly sliced
Thick yogurt 5–6 tablespoons
Water 2 tablespoons
Ground cinnamon ½ teaspoon
Fresh mint a few leaves
Fresh coriander a few sprigs

Pickled whole baby aubergines
Ravaiyya baingan achari

There are several varieties of aubergine, or 'brinjal' as we call them in India. The baby, rounded variety is commonly found in either white or purple and both are equally good to use. You could also use the thin, long ones, either whole or cut in half if too long. Pickling in almost every region of India is common – what is different is the style, method or the spice that dominates in different regions. Serve these aubergines with warm chapattis.

1   Heat the rapeseed oil in a wok or a kadhai over a medium heat, add the onion and sauté until well browned, about 6–7 minutes. Drain in a sieve set over a bowl. The best way to drain fried onions is to press them against the side of the sieve and leave the centre empty for the oil to drip into the bowl below.

2   Place ½ teaspoon of the salt in a small bowl with the water and stir until dissolved. Add the turmeric, fennel, lime juice and ground coriander. Stir to make a paste and set aside.

3   Wipe the wok or kadhai clean, add the mustard oil and place over a high heat. When making a tempering use a wok-like pan as this will allow you to use less oil.

4   Reduce the heat and add the mustard seeds. Stir-fry for 30 seconds or until the seeds start to crackle. Add the remaining salt and the spice paste and cook until the water evaporates and oil appears at the base of the pan. When this happens, add the onion, mix well and taste, then add the fresh coriander and remove from the heat.

5   Preheat the oven to 140°C/275°F/Gas Mark 1.

6   Fill the middle of the aubergines with equal amounts of the mixture. Press the splits together to hold the filling inside. You can also gently tie them with thin string, if you like.

7   With a brush or using your hands, rub the drained onion oil on to the skin of the aubergines and place on a small baking tray. Bake until soft but not browned; they won't take long, about 8–10 minutes. Turn them once or twice while cooking.

8   Serve the aubergines with yogurt mixed with mint, coriander and lime juice, if you like. Top with peanuts to add texture.

Serves 4–6

Extra-virgin rapeseed oil 3–5 tablespoons
Red onions 4–5 small, chopped
Sea salt 1 teaspoon
Water 4–5 tablespoons
Ground turmeric ½ teaspoon
Fennel seeds 1½ teaspoons, crushed
Lime juice from ½–1 lime
Ground coriander 1 heaped teaspoon
Mustard oil 4 tablespoons
Black mustard seeds 1 teaspoon
Fresh coriander a few sprigs, chopped
Baby aubergines 6–8 or 3–4 slender ones, stems left attached and slit into 4

To serve
Yogurt
Fresh mint a few sprigs, chopped
Fresh coriander a few sprigs, chopped
Lime juice a drizzle (optional)
Roasted peanuts roughly chopped (optional)

Notes
I like to add a squeeze of lime or lemon juice and some jaggery or raw cane sugar to the tempering.
   You can also mix together a little turmeric and red chilli powder and rub it into the slits of the aubergine.

Courgette, potato & butternut squash koftas in a creamy coconut & tomato sauce
Lauki, kaddu and aloo kofta

Koftas are dumplings generally served in a sauce. Here is a simple recipe that you can make, but you can also adapt it and use whatever other vegetables you have available to bring it all together. You will likely have some koftas left over, so keep these separate from the sauce and serve them fried as a snack to eat with a dipping sauce. Pictured overleaf.

1   In a large bowl, mix together all the kofta ingredients, except for the oil, and knead to make a dough. If it is too soft or sticky, add more rice flour.

2   Heat 5cm (2in) oil in a deep pan over a low heat and fry a small piece of the vegetable mixture to see if it does not disintegrate. If it does, add a bit more flour to bind.

3   Roll the dough into golf-ball-sized balls and fry in batches until nice and golden brown, about 4–5 minutes. Remove with a slotted spoon and place on a plate lined with kitchen peper to drain.

4   To make the sauce, mix the ginger & garlic paste and the dry spices with the water until smooth and well combined.

5   Heat the oil in a saucepan and add the bay leaves and cinnamon. In about 30 seconds, when the leaves sizzle and the cinnamon swells a bit, add the spice paste and sauté until the liquid dries up and the oil begins to appear at the edges of the pan.

6   Add the crushed tomatoes and let cook for 10–15 minutes over a medium heat, until the tomatoes thicken. When that happens, add the coconut milk and bring it to a simmer, then cook for 5–7 minutes until thick and creamy.

7   Turn off the heat and set aside to cool slightly. Remove the cinnamon and bay leaves. Place in a blender and blitz until the sauce has a smooth consistency.

Serves 4

For the koftas
Courgette or marrow 300–400g (10½–14oz), grated
Boiled potatoes 300–400g (10½–14oz), peeled and grated
Butternut squash 300–400g (10½–14oz), peeled and grated
Chickpea (gram) flour 4–5 tablespoons
Rice flour 3–4 tablespoons
Spring onions 2, finely chopped
Onion 1 small, chopped
Chopped fresh ginger 2 heaped teaspoons
Chopped garlic 1 teaspoon
Cumin seeds 1 teaspoon, crushed
Fresh green chillies 2, finely chopped
Chopped fresh coriander 1–2 tablespoons
Freshly ground black pepper ½ teaspoon
Salt ½ teaspoon
Oil for deep-frying

8   Pour the sauce back into the saucepan, clean out the blender with a little water and add this water to the sauce to thin it down slightly.

9   Add the lime juice and some seasoning.

10 Either add the koftas to the sauce just before serving or serve the koftas with the sauce poured over the top. This is delicious served with some rice.

For the sauce

Ginger & garlic paste (see page 188) 1½ tablespoons
Ground coriander 1 tablespoon
Ground turmeric ¼–½ teaspoon
Garam masala (see page 186) ½ teaspoon
Red chilli powder 1 heaped teaspoon
Water 150ml (5fl oz)
Oil 2 tablespoons
Bay leaves 2–3
Cinnamon stick 5cm (2in) piece
Tomatoes 300–400g (10½–14oz), pulped, or tin of chopped tomatoes 1 x 400g (14oz)
Coconut milk 1 x 400ml (14fl oz) tin
Lime juice from ½ lime

Parsee-style wedding stew
Khattu mitthu lagan nu stew

We Parsees are not known for our vegetarian dishes. Eggs, yes. Vegetables, no!
I know many that will not even touch a green pea and in many cases we destroy
the very element of a vegetable by cooking it to death. So this is a rare and yet
flavourful dish, which used to be served often at weddings, hence the name
'wedding stew'. Enjoy with some chapattis.

1   Soak the jaggery or sugar in the vinegar along with the
    sultanas and dates.

2   Heat the majority of the oil in a frying pan over a medium
    heat. One vegetable at a time, fry the carrot, the sweet
    potato, the potato and the yam until nicely browned, then
    transfer to a tray lined with kitchen paper to let drain. Frying
    will stop the vegetables from becoming too mushy and soft.

3   Place the tomato and onion in a blender and blitz to a purée,
    or chop as finely as possible.

4   Add the remaining oil to a casserole dish placed over a
    medium heat.

5   Put the ginger & garlic paste in a small bowl, add the
    turmeric, cardamom and chilli powders and a few tablespoons
    of water and mix to form a paste. When the oil in the pan is
    reasonably hot, add this paste with the curry leaves and
    sauté until the paste dries out and starts to release more oil.

6   As soon as that happens, add the onion and tomato pulp and
    continue cooking for 8–10 minutes, until the pulp becomes
    thick and sticky. Use a flat spatula to stir regularly and
    scrape the bottom of the pan. When little bubbles of oil
    appear, add the sultana and date mixture along with the
    nutmeg and cook for 3–4 minutes.

7   Add a little water, if needed, to keep the mixture from drying
    out completely. Stir in the fried vegetables and the peas and
    add the pepper and some salt. If the vegetables are not quite
    cooked through, cover the pan to create some steam in order
    to cook further. Cook until the vegetables are done and still
    have some crunch. Fold in the coriander and serve.

Serves 4

Jaggery or raw cane sugar 100g (3½oz)
   (or dark brown sugar 50g (2oz))
Cider or cane vinegar 150ml (5fl oz)
Sultanas 2 heaped tablespoons
Seedless dates 8–10, chopped
Oil 150–200ml (5–7fl oz)
Carrots 2–3, peeled and cubed
Sweet potatoes 2, peeled and cubed
Potatoes 3, peeled and cubed
Yam 1 small, peeled and cubed (or turnip,
   swede or tapioca)
Tomatoes 4–5, roughly chopped
Onions 3–4, roughly chopped
Ginger & garlic paste (see page 188)
   1 tablespoon
Ground turmeric 1 heaped teaspoon
Ground cardamom ¼ teaspoon
Red chilli powder 1 heaped tablespoon
Curry leaves 15–20, preferably fresh,
   shredded; if using dried, soak in water
   for 10–12 minutes, and dry thoroughly
   before shredding
Grated nutmeg ¼ teaspoon
Green peas 200g (7oz), fresh or frozen,
   blanched if fresh (see page 23)
White pepper 2 teaspoons
Chopped fresh coriander 2 heaped
   tablespoons
Salt

Mixed mushrooms with onion, red chilli & ginger
Dhingri milavut do pyaza laal mirich

This is a simple preparation that is very different to what you might find in a restaurant – it is quick and does not need a lot of planning or preparation. It's best if you use one large frying pan or casserole dish for this.

1   Soak the dried chillies in a little water and vinegar for 2 minutes.

2   Meanwhile, heat a heavy-based frying pan over a high heat. Keep on the heat for about 2 minutes in order for it to become really hot. Wash the mushrooms and drain in a sieve set over a bowl. Shake the mushrooms to get rid of any droplets of water, otherwise they will splutter and make the pan cold. Add the oil (it may start to smoke immediately), then tilt the pan to spread the oil and add in the mushrooms. Do not shake the mushrooms except to level them out.

3   After about 30 seconds, toss the mushrooms, but maintain the high heat. Do this by gently mixing, and then allow the moisture to evaporate. A minute or so later the mushrooms will be done. Drain in a sieve, again over the bowl collecting the liquid.

4   Melt the butter in the same pan over a medium heat, add the fennel seeds and when they give off an aroma, add the drained soaked red chillies and sauté for about a minute. Add the green chilli and ginger and sauté for 2–3 minutes, then remove with a slotted spoon into a bowl.

5   Reheat the pan over a medium heat, add the onion and stir-fry until it turns pale, about 3–4 minutes. Stir in the tomato and any drained mushroom liquid collected and cook until nearly dry.

6   Add the mushrooms and the chilli mixture and stir until combined. Increase the heat to high, season, then cook for about 2 minutes until hot and all the moisture has evaporated.

7   Turn off the heat and gently stir in the mint. Cover for a minute or two before serving.

Serves 4

Dried red chillies 3 large, deseeded, cut into strips and washed well
Vinegar a dash
Mixed mushrooms 400–500g (14oz–1lb 2oz), trimmed and roughly chopped
Oil 1 tablespoon
Butter 2 tablespoons
Fennel seeds ½ teaspoon
Fresh green chillies 2 finger-type, slit in half and cut into 4
Fresh ginger 5–7.5cm (2–3in) piece, peeled and thinly sliced
Onions 3–4 small, diced into roughly 1cm (½in) pieces
Tomato 1 large, pulp removed and flesh diced
Fresh mint 6–8 leaves, torn
Salt and freshly ground black pepper

7

PULSES
- & -
GRAINS

*

Whole pink lentils with black-eye beans
Akkha masoor ma chora

Parsees do love their lentils and beans and they will often form the basis of a meal. This is simple, tasty, rich in protein and very wholesome, and there are several versions of it, as one would expect. To enjoy, serve with a red onion salad or cachumber (see page 177) and some warm chapattis. Whenever lentils and pulses are cooked, a decent blob of ghee or butter will help to enhance the flavour.

1   Rinse the masoor or lentils and the beans, then soak separately. Use slightly warm water, covering 2–3cm (1in) above the pulse, soaking for 3–4 hours or overnight.

2   Separately cook the pulses in boiling water. The masoor or lentils will take about 30–40 minutes and the black-eye beans about 2 hours. Once cooked, turn off the heat. If there is a lot of excess liquid, drain in a colander set over a bowl.

3   Gently crush the masoor or lentils with the reverse of a ladle or potato masher and mix into the beans.

4   Heat any collected cooking water in a casserole dish over a medium heat and reduce. Add the pulses and turn the heat down to a simmer.

5   Meanwhile, in a large frying pan, heat the oil. Add the cumin, ginger, garlic and green chilli and sauté until the garlic is lightly coloured, about 2 minutes.

6   Add the butter and the onion and cook until the onion starts to colour, about 5–6 minutes. Add the tomato and cook for another 5–6 minutes. Add this all to the daal mixture and blend in well. Season, sprinkle over the coriander and serve.

Serves 4

Whole masoor or puy lentils
   150g (5½oz)
Black-eye beans (lobia) 250g (9oz)
Oil 1 tablespoon
Cumin seeds 2 teaspoons
Finely chopped fresh ginger
   1 tablespoon
Garlic 4–5 cloves, chopped
Fresh green chillies 1–2, chopped
Butter 2 heaped tablespoons
Red onions 2 small, chopped
Tomato 1 large, chopped
Chopped fresh coriander
   1–2 tablespoons
Salt

Split mung bean & rice pulao
Mug ni daal ni khichdi

Khichdis or khichris are simple, easy meals that are wholesome, filling, easily digestible and, most importantly, soul satisfying. Every mum in India has her own version and young kids always claim that their mum's is the best! My mother loved to drop a nice dollop of butter in hers.

1   Rinse and soak the rice and beans together in some water for about 30 minutes. Drain well.

2   Preheat the oven to 140°C/275°F/Gas Mark 1.

3   Over a medium heat, warm the oil or ghee in a casserole dish that has a lid and that can be placed in the oven. Once the oil is hot, add the cumin seeds and in 30 seconds, once they change colour slightly, add the ginger, garlic and green chilli and sauté until the garlic changes colour, about 2 minutes. Add the onion and sauté well until the onion turns pale, about 3–4 minutes, then add the chopped tomato and the turmeric. Sauté until the tomato turns to pulp and almost dries out, about 8–10 minutes, then add the water and salt.

4   When the water comes to a boil, add the rice and daal mix and stir regularly until the water starts to be absorbed. When this happens, clean down the sides of the dish with a flat spatula, add some seasoning, cover the dish and place in the oven.

5   Let cook for 10–12 minutes, then turn off the oven and leave the dish inside for another 30 minutes or so. Remove, stir gently and check the seasoning. Sometimes, depending on the rice, the khichdi can become dry and lumpy. If this has happened, add some water and stir to get a porridge-like consistency.

6   Sprinkle with some coriander, if you like, and serve.

Serves 3–4

Rice 250g (9oz) (no glutinous-types)
Split mung beans (mung daal) 120g (4oz)
Oil or ghee 2 tablespoons
Cumin seeds 1 teaspoon
Fresh ginger 2.5cm (1in) piece, peeled and finely chopped
Garlic 2 cloves, finely chopped
Fresh green chillies 1–2, finely chopped
Onion 1 medium, finely chopped
Tomato 1, chopped
Ground turmeric ½ teaspoon
Hot water 500ml (18fl oz)
Salt ¾ teaspoon
Freshly ground black pepper
Fresh coriander to serve, chopped (optional)

Note
You could also add:
- Diced vegetables, added with the rice and daal.
- Curry leaves, added with the cumin seeds (as shown).
- Crushed coriander seeds, added with the ginger.

Creamy black urad daal
Daal makhani, maa ki daal or kaali daal

Some families are fanatical about their daal, as are some chefs, and there is always some argument or other about whose maa ki daal or daal makhani is better. I lay claim to no such argument, but we do know that we make a mean one, even if it is slightly different to most others. I go by my own taste buds, sticking as close to tradition as possible. Serve hot with naan or soft pilau rice.

1   Rinse the whole black urad beans, then cover in slightly warm water about 5cm (2in) above the surface, and soak in a warm place overnight.

2   When the black beans are well soaked and expanded, gently rub them between the palms of your hands to remove some of the outer husks. These will float to the surface when washed, so lift out, discard and wash the beans well. There will be some white- or grey-looking beans and some that are still whole. This will create a rich and creamy texture.

3   Combine the beans in a deep casserole dish, adding 2.5–5cm (1–2in) water above the surface, then bring gently to the boil. Remove any scum that comes to the surface and reduce the heat to a simmer. Add a little salt.

4   Cook the beans for 1 hour until thoroughly cooked and the red kidney beans can easily be mashed.

5   Gently heat the butter and oil in a saucepan. As soon as the butter has melted, add the cumin seeds and stir until they change colour, about 30 seconds. Add the ginger, garlic and green chilli and sauté until the garlic turns a pale brown, about 2–3 minutes.

6   Add the onion and the chilli powder and sauté until the onion turns pale or light brown and the fat separates at the bottom, about 3–4 minutes. Add the tomatoes and cook until they turn soft and pulpy, about 4–5 minutes, then add the cooked beans. Stir well, bring to a soft boil and season.

7   Check the seasoning. Pour into bowls, drizzle over the cream and sprinkle over the garam masala, if using, just before serving.

Serves 4–6 as a side

Whole black urad beans 200–250g (7–9oz)
Red kidney beans 1 x 400g (14oz) tin, drained
Butter 3–4 tablespoons
Oil 1 tablespoon
Cumin seeds 1½ teaspoons
Fresh ginger 2 x 5cm (2in) pieces, peeled and very finely sliced
Garlic 4–5 cloves, finely chopped
Fresh green chillies 2–3 finger-type, sliced in 4 lengthways
Red onions 2
Red chilli powder 1 heaped teaspoon
Plum tomatoes 2–3, roughly chopped
Single cream 3–4 tablespoons
Garam masala (see page 186) 1 teaspoon (optional)
Salt and freshly ground black pepper

Chickpea masala
Channa masala or masalaydaar cholay

From the Punjab originally, this dish is prepared across India and made in a thousand different ways, but it is always popular when served with hot fried poori or bhaturas (poori made using fermented white flour dough). This recipe will also suit all kinds of chickpeas, from the large white to the small black or brown and even the very typical Italian 'ceci neri' from Sicily, which are black. Serve with bread or rice, with a red onion and tomato salad and some lime wedges.

1   Heat the oil in a wok or a deep casserole dish over a medium heat. Fry the ginger & garlic paste and the green chilli for about 2–3 minutes. Add the onion and sauté until it turns a light brown, 4–5 minutes.

2   Meanwhile, mix half the channa masala with the turmeric and chilli powder along with a little of the chickpea liquid from the tin (keep the rest for later). It should be the consistency of single cream.

3   Once the onion is cooked, add the chopped tomatoes and garam masala and cook until most of the moisture dries out, about 5–6 minutes, then add the masala paste and cook until the liquid evaporates. Add a little butter.

4   Cook the masala for about 12–15 minutes or until the oil starts to emerge from the thick sauce. Add the chickpeas and stir in well, crushing a few to thicken the sauce further. Mix in the rest of the liquid from the tin of chickpeas and cook until heated through. Taste and add the rest of the channa masala, if needed.

5   Season, add some coriander and lime juice and serve.

Serves 4–5 as a side

Oil 2–3 tablespoons
Ginger & garlic paste (see page 188) 2 teaspoons
Fresh green chillies 2–3, chopped
Onion 1, finely chopped
Channa masala (see page 190) 1 tablespoon
Ground turmeric ½ teaspoon
Red chilli powder 1 teaspoon
Chickpeas 2 x 400g (14oz) tins
Tomatoes 2, finely chopped
Garam masala (see page 186) ¼ teaspoon
Butter
Chopped fresh coriander 1 heaped tablespoon
Lime juice to taste
Salt

Yogurt rice with cucumber, tomato & fried peanuts
Tamatar kakdi our moonphalli ka dahi bhaat

If I ever have any leftover rice in the fridge, my immediate thought is to make a bowl of this. It is a really surprising dish that is fragrant and delicious, and even if you don't have any cooked rice to hand and need to start from scratch, it won't take any time at all to make. This will very simply satisfy your soul and is a great cure for when you are feeling low and don't have a great appetite.

Serves 4

1   If cooking the rice, cook according to the packet instructions, drain and cool. Refrigerate once cooled to chill completely.

2   Place the coriander, chilli powder and turmeric in a small bowl and make a thin paste with the water. Cover and set aside.

3   Heat the oil in a frying pan over a medium heat. Fry the peanuts for a minute or so, stirring regularly, then drain in a sieve placed over a bowl. Return the oil to the frying pan and heat again.

4   Once the oil is hot and hazy, add the mustard seeds and cover the pan loosely to prevent them from popping all over the place. As soon as they start to settle in the pan, add the cumin seeds, the white lentils, curry leaves and the green chilli and cook until the daal changes colour. Immediately add the asafoetida powder, if using, sauté for a few seconds, then add this tadka mixture to the yogurt, scraping the pan.

5   Add the onion, tomato and cucumber to the yogurt and mix well. Stir in the fresh coriander and some seasoning.

6   Mix the rice into the yogurt and taste for seasoning. Some people like to add a bit of sugar at this point, but it is completely optional.

7   Serve the rice cold, topped with the fried peanuts.

Cold boiled rice 500g (1lb 2oz) or uncooked rice 200g (7oz)
Ground coriander 1 teaspoon
Ground turmeric ½ teaspoon
Red chilli powder 1 teaspoon
Oil 3–4 tablespoons
Unskinned peanuts 150–200g (5½–7oz)
Black mustard seeds 1 teaspoon
Cumin seeds 1 teaspoon
White lentils (urad daal) 1 tablespoon
Curry leaves 10–15, preferably fresh, shredded; if using dried, soak in water for 10–12 minutes, and dry thoroughly before shredding
Fresh green chillies 2–3, roughly chopped
Asafoetida ¼ teaspoon (optional)
Greek-style yogurt 450g (1lb), beaten
Red onion 1 small, chopped
Tomatoes 2, pulp discarded and flesh chopped
Cucumber ½, cored and diced
Chopped fresh coriander 1 heaped tablespoon
Sugar (optional)
Salt

Quinoa & mushroom tadka

Quinoa has become very popular across the world of late and Britain is no exception. With its demand rising, it is only fair that a British farmer tries their hand at growing it and I am pleased to say that in the Cotswolds we now grow our very own British quinoa. Since I do quite a bit of work with this farmer, I was recently sent a sample of smoked quinoa, which I used in a simple dish and thought it was amazing. It was strange at first and then its flavour began to actually take better shape and gave a great deal of enjoyment to those who tried it. This is that simple recipe and it took me minutes to put it together. Use plain or smoked quinoa.

1   Soak the quinoa in warm water up to 2.5cm (1in) above the surface for 15–20 minutes. Boil for 8–10 minutes on a gentle rolling boil and drain.

2   Heat 1 tablespoon of oil in a large frying pan until smoking and add the sliced mushrooms. Do not stir for a few seconds. Then toss them briefly as you do not want all the juices to escape.

3   Add the onion, squeeze in the lime and sauté together until the onion turns soft and pale, about 3–4 minutes. Add the tomato, sautéing for a minute or so, then take off the heat and set aside in a bowl.

4   Wipe out the frying pan and add the remaining oil to it. Place over a medium heat and add the mustard seeds, keeping a loose lid held over to protect from the popping seeds. As soon as the crackling lessens, lower the heat, add the lentils and stir until the colour changes, then immediately add the cumin seeds and curry leaves.

5   When the cumin changes colour, after about 30 seconds, add the green chilli and ginger and sauté for a minute. Stir in the quinoa and let it warm through slowly. Add some seasoning.

6   Mix in the coriander and serve warm.

Serves 3–4 as a side

Quinoa 200g (7oz)
Oil 3 tablespoons
Button mushrooms 150–200g (5½–7oz), sliced
Onion 1, finely chopped
Lime juice from ½ lime
Plum tomatoes 2, diced
Black mustard seeds 1½ teaspoons
White lentils (urad daal) 2 teaspoons
Cumin seeds 1 teaspoon
Curry leaves 12–15, preferably fresh, shredded or chopped; if using dried, soak in water for 10–12 minutes, and dry thoroughly before shredding or chopping
Fresh green chillies 2 finger-type, finely chopped
Fresh ginger 5cm (2in) piece, peeled and finely chopped
Chopped fresh coriander 1 tablespoon
Salt

Cumin, red chilli & garlic risotto
Arroz refogado suave com comino

This rice is different to the usual al dente style of cooking risotto. However, with curries and other thin Indian sauces, this version works much better and overall gives a much softer texture.

1   Heat the oil and butter in a saucepan over a medium heat and add the cumin seeds. When the seeds release their aroma and change colour slightly, about 30 seconds, add the garlic and red chilli and sauté until the garlic changes colour, about 2 minutes. Add the green chilli.

2   Stir in the onion and cook until it turns pale, about 3–4 minutes. Add the rice and cook for 10–15 minutes over a medium heat, making sure to not let the vegetables or rice burn.

3   Start adding a little of the stock at a time, allowing the liquid to be absorbed before adding another spoonful. Cook until the risotto has a soft consistency, no bite and the rice is still whole.

4   Meanwhile, add a little oil to a frying pan over a medium heat. Add the peppers and cook for 5–6 minutes until cooked.

5   When the rice is ready, add the peppers and sprinkle over some coriander just before serving.

Serves 6–8

Olive oil 150ml (5fl oz), plus a little extra for the peppers
Butter 150g (5½oz)
Cumin seeds 2–3 teaspoons
Garlic 6–8 cloves, chopped
Dried red chillies 4, cut into thin strips
Fresh green chillies 2 finger-type, chopped
Red onions 2, finely chopped
Risotto rice 500g (1lb 2oz)
Vegetable stock 1.5 litres (2¾ pints)
Spring onions 3–4, chopped
Green pepper 1, chopped
Red pepper 1, chopped
Fresh coriander chopped, to serve

Chickpeas & yellow split peas with red onion
Cholay channa daal do pyazza

This dish is very simple and easy to make and will delight most palates. You can use either tinned chickpeas or soaked dried chickpeas. This can also be cooked without the whole spices if you so wish. Serve with warm flatbreads such as chapattis, parathas, Turkish flatbreads or naan, as an accompaniment to a meal or with steamed rice and a fresh red onion and mint salad.

1 Soak the yellow split peas for 3 hours and then cook in boiling water for about 40 minutes, or until just soft but not overcooked. Drain in a colander set over a bowl.

2 Over a medium heat, warm the oil in a deep casserole dish roughly 23cm (9in) in diameter. Add the cinnamon, bay leaves, peppercorns and, after 10–15 seconds, the cumin seeds. Turn the heat down a little.

3 As soon as the cumin changes colour, about 30 seconds, add the ginger, garlic, green chilli and the butter and sauté until the garlic colours slightly, about 2 minutes. Stir in the onion and continue to sauté over a medium heat for 5–6 minutes or until a pale brown.

4 Meanwhile, put the turmeric, chilli powder and coriander powder in a small bowl and add enough water to make a thin paste.

5 Once the onion is golden, add the spice paste and stir well. Cook until the liquid dries up and tiny beads of oil start emerging at the bottom of the dish. Add the yellow split peas and chickpeas, the reserved cooking water and the tomato and simmer until the sauce is thick and the pulses are well coated in the sauce, about 10 minutes.

6 Stir in the seasoning and the garam masala, top with the fresh coriander and serve.

Serves 4 as a side

Yellow split peas (channa daal) 150g (5½oz)
Oil 2 tablespoons
Cinnamon stick 5–8cm (2–3in) piece
Bay leaves 2
Peppercorns 5–6, cracked
Cumin seeds 1 heaped teaspoon
Fresh ginger 5–8cm (2–3in) piece, peeled and finely chopped
Garlic 4–5 cloves, finely chopped
Fresh green chillies 2–3 finger-type, slit into 4 lengthways
Butter 2 tablespoons
Onions 2 small, finely chopped
Ground turmeric ½ teaspoon
Red chilli powder 1 teaspoon
Ground coriander 1 tablespoon
Tinned chickpeas 150g (5½oz)
Tomatoes 2, chopped
Garam masala (see page 186) ½ teaspoon
Chopped fresh coriander 2 heaped tablespoons
Salt

Summer green palav
Hariyali palav

A simple palav using a basic South-Indian-style of preparing rice, flavouring it with cumin and cracked mustard seeds. I like using sliced coconut for this rice as it adds to the texture, but it isn't essential. For the vegetables, use what you think will work best or what you have in your fridge, but always look for new and seasonal vegetables to add taste, texture and variety to the dish. Pictured overleaf.

1   To make the stock for the rice, pour the water into a saucepan and bring to the boil. Add a little salt and, one by one, blanch the vegetables until cooked but retaining a bit of bite and not soft. Use a slotted spoon to lift each of the vegetables out of the water and transfer to a sieve placed over a bowl. Leave to cool and reserve the water.

2   Measure 1 litre (1¾ pints) of the reserved water, topping up with fresh water if there isn't enough. Pour the cooking water back into the pan.

3   Preheat the oven to 130°C/260°F/Gas Mark ¾.

4   Heat the oil in a large pot or casserole dish that has a lid and can go in the oven. Add the mustard seeds and cinnamon stick. As soon as the mustard seeds crackle, add the cumin seeds and red chilli and, after a few seconds, the curry leaves, ginger and onion.

5   As soon as the onion turns soft, about 3–4 minutes, add the sliced coconut and the turmeric and sauté for a couple of minutes until the coconut starts to change colour slightly around the edges.

6   Add the vegetable stock and bring to the boil. Check the seasoning and add more salt if needed. Pour in the rice and stir gently with a flat wooden spatula to prevent it from sticking to the bottom. Cook for 5–6 minutes, until the water is nearly absorbed. Stir in the vegetables, cover the pot and place in the oven.

7   Cook for 15 minutes or so, then turn the oven off and leave the palav in the oven for another 10–12 minutes. Remove and mix together gently. Check the rice to make sure that it is cooked and is not too hard.

8   Serve the rice immediately with some daal or yogurt or even on its own.

Serves 4–6

Water 1.25 litres (2¼ pints)
Fresh or frozen broad beans 200g (7oz), skinned
Broccoli ½ head, cut into florets and the stalks sliced
Kale 2 handfuls, chopped
Potato 1 large, diced
Fresh or frozen green peas 100g (3½oz)
Oil 3 tablespoons
Black mustard seeds 1 teaspoon
Cinnamon stick 2cm (¾in) piece
Cumin seeds 1 teaspoon
Dried red chillies 2 large, chopped
Curry leaves 12–15, preferably fresh, shredded; if using dried, soak in water for 10–12 minutes, and dry thoroughly before shredding
Fresh ginger 5cm (2in) piece, peeled and chopped
Onion 1, sliced
Coconut flesh from ¼ coconut, freshly sliced (optional)
Ground turmeric ½ teaspoon
Basmati rice 500g (1lb 2oz)
Salt

8

DESSERTS

❋

Parsee fudge cake
Parsee mawa cake

Mawa or khoya is nothing but milk reduced to the extent of it becoming solid. It is used in fillings for various dishes, blended into sweets such as fudge, and here it is added to a cake mix to give a nutty, caramelized milk flavour. The original mawa cake is synonymous in Bombay with a particular café called B Meherwan, whose mawa cakes are famous and enjoyed with tea.

1   Preheat the oven to 180°C/350°F/Gas Mark 4 and line a 15–20cm (6–8in) cake tin with baking parchment.

2   Sift the flour, baking powder and the ground green cardamom together and set aside.

3   In another bowl or food processor, beat together the khoya, sugar and butter until the mixture is light and fluffy and pale in colour. Add the eggs gradually to the mix, then the condensed milk.

4   In three stages, add a third of the flour mix and a tablespoon of the milk and then whisk to combine. Repeat until you have a smooth batter. If it is too thick, add an extra tablespoon or two of milk to make it a pourable consistency. Blend in the vanilla.

5   Pour the mixture into the tin, level it out, then sprinkle both of the chopped nuts on top.

6   Bake in the centre of the oven for about 40–45 minutes or until done. The top should be golden and when the centre is pierced with a thin knife it should come out clean.

7   Let cool slightly in the tin. When ready to serve, remove from the tin and serve warm with some tea.

Serves 6

Plain flour 160g (5¾ oz)
Baking powder ½ teaspoon
Green cardamom pods 4–5, seeds finely ground
Khoya/mawa 100g (3½oz), crumbled (**or use gulab jamuns** 4–5, from an Indian sweet shop – just squeeze out the excess syrup before adding)
Caster sugar 150g (5½oz)
Salted butter 100g (3½oz)
Eggs 2 large, at room temperature, beaten
Condensed milk 3 tablespoons
Full-fat milk 3 tablespoons
Vanilla extract ¼ teaspoon
Chopped almonds 1 heaped tablespoon
Pistachios 10–12, chopped

Banana bread & butter pudding
Kaeda nay paav nu pudding

The pan-fried bananas added to this pudding give it a unique taste. I remember the very first time I ever made this was when I worked in Switzerland many years ago in the pastry kitchen of the Geneva Intercontinental. It was a trial to develop, but it proved to be very successful, so I hope you enjoy it too. This is a Parsee-style recipe and you will notice that we do not hold back on calories when a great dessert is being made. You may serve tiny portions if you like, of course. Ideally, the dish should be soaked in the milk a day in advance, and then baked on the day of eating.

1   Peel and slit the bananas in half lengthways.

2   Heat 5mm (¼in) of oil in a large frying pan over a medium heat and fry the bananas, first rounded side down and then flat side down. Remove from the pan once you have a good caramelized colour on both sides and place on a plate lined with some kitchen paper to drain.

3   Take a large casserole dish and butter it with the 1 tablespoon of the butter. Coat the inside of the entire dish with sugar.

4   Butter one side of half of the slices of bread and place them buttered-side down in the base of the dish. Press them down firmly and fill any gaps with smaller pieces of buttered bread. Butter the top of the bread as best you can, using a brush or spatula.

5   Beat the marmalade in a small bowl to soften and make it looser and easier to apply. Smear the marmalade on top of the buttered slices, then arrange the banana halves to cover as much of the bread as is possible. Sprinkle over the sultanas.

6   In a large bowl, mix together the evaporated milk, condensed milk, the eggs, egg yolks and the flavourings. Beat well. You can add or adjust the flavours here if you like – for example a little more cardamom. Pour enough of the mixture over the bananas just to cover.

7   Cut the remaining bread slices into triangles, butter both sides and place on top of the bananas, arranging the triangles to sit so that they overlap each other. Press down gently to flatten slightly, then slowly pour most of the remaining mixture over the bread. Place the dish in the fridge for a few hours to rest or overnight. Keep an eye on the dish, and as the liquid is absorbed top up with more of the mixture until it is completely saturated.

Serves 6–8

Bananas 6
Oil for frying
Salted butter 1 tablespoon, plus
    extra for spreading
Sugar 1–2 tablespoons
White bread (or brioche)
    10–14 slices
Orange marmalade
    3–4 tablespoons
Sultanas 3–4 tablespoons
Evaporated milk 3 x 400ml
    (14fl oz) tins
Condensed milk 1 x 400ml
    (14fl oz) tin
Eggs 6, plus egg yolks 6
Green cardamom pods
    4–5, seeds finely ground
Grated nutmeg ¼ teaspoon
Rosewater 2 teaspoons
Vanilla extract ¼ teaspoon

Continued overleaf

8 Preheat the oven to 150°C/300°F/Gas Mark 2.

9 Place the casserole dish in a deep baking tray. Transfer both to the middle shelf of the oven and carefully pour boiling water into the deep baking tray so that it sits along the sides. However, make sure that the water does not get into the pudding or that the tray is filled too high. Bake for 20–30 minutes until golden on top. When the centre is pierced with a thin knife the pudding should feel set. Once set, remove the tray from the oven and place the dish on a tea towel to dry the base. At this point, if you prefer the top of the pudding to be well-browned and crisp, put the dish back into the oven on the top shelf for a few minutes.

10 Once cooked, let cool slightly and serve warm with some fresh cream or some fresh or stewed fruits.

Lemon, orange & fennel scones
Limbu, santra aur saunf ka paav

We recently started a once-a-month afternoon tea with influences from Bombay and the gymkhanas that still adhere to the tradition of a great afternoon tea service. This recipe emerged during one such session, when trying to give the traditional scone an Indian twist. Clotted cream was something we all grew up with as cream was not pasteurized and had to be boiled. The cream that floated to the surface was collected and served at breakfast or tea with toast, butter and jam.

1   Preheat the oven to 220°C/425°F/Gas Mark 7. Lightly grease a large baking tray.

2   Sift the flour, salt and baking powder into a large mixing bowl and mix in the zests and fennel seeds. Use your fingertips to gently rub the butter into the flour until well mixed in.

3   Add the sugar and lightly mix, then make a well in the middle. Pour in the milk and gradually bring the flour into the middle and mix to make a dough. Be careful not to overmix, and, if needed, add a tiny bit more milk to bring the dough together.

4   Dust the work surface with flour and knead very lightly to bring the dough into a ball. Gently roll out the dough to approximately 2cm (¾in) thick. Cut out using a 5cm (2in) or 4cm (1½in) round cutter. Place them close together on the baking tray.

5   Brush the tops with milk and bake for 12–15 minutes or until well risen and golden on top.

6   Serve hot, either plain or with the accompaniments of your choice. I avoid the arguments of Devon, Dorset and Cornwall as to what comes first: the cream or the jam. Just enjoy and decide for yourself.

Makes 12–14 scones

Butter 70g (2½oz), diced, plus extra for greasing
Self-raising flour 250g (9oz), plus extra for dusting
Salt a good pinch
Baking powder ½ teaspoon
Grated orange zest from ½ orange
Grated lime zest from ½–¾ lime
Fennel seeds ½ teaspoon, crushed
Caster sugar 40g (1½oz)
Cold milk 160ml (5½fl oz), plus a little for brushing

To serve (optional)
Clotted cream
Mixed fruit jam
Butter

Chocolate & courgette cake à la Edi Csanalosi
Chocolate aur lauki ka cake

Edi is the nutritionist we have been working with for a while. She has tried very hard to make the Café Spice Namasté team eat healthier and better. Less sugar and low on carbs – all the usual stuff. And do we listen... No! We Asians are too deeply rooted in our bad habits. But then she hosted an entire day of nutrition and I made this cake for the morning break. Unusual, but really nice! Not as healthy as Edi would have liked, but then I did cut it into smallish squares...

1   Preheat the oven to 180°C/350°F/Gas Mark 4. Line a 33 x 23cm (13 x 9in) baking tin with baking parchment.

2   Trim and grate the courgettes using the fattest grater available, then place in a clean tea towel or muslin and squeeze out as much of the water as possible. Leave in a sieve until needed.

3   Using an electric whisk or stand mixer, beat together the sugar and butter until light and creamy. While still mixing, add the vanilla and the eggs and continue to beat for a minute or so.

4   In a separate bowl, mix together the two flours, cocoa powder, baking powder, cardamom, cinnamon and nutmeg.

5   Gently fold the dry mixture into the wet ingredients using a metal spoon. Stir in the courgettes until well combined. Pour the mixture into the baking tin and level out. Bake for 30 minutes, until it feels firm when the top is pressed. Remove from the oven and leave to cool.

6   Cut into squares once completely cool and serve.

Makes 9–12 squares

Courgettes 500g (1lb 2oz)
Dark brown sugar 220g (8oz)
Butter 150g (5½oz), softened
Vanilla extract 2 teaspoons
Eggs 4, beaten
Milk 150ml (5fl oz)
Plain flour 250g (9oz)
Wholemeal flour 100g (3½oz)
Cocoa powder 75g (2½oz)
Baking powder 2 teaspoons
Ground cardamom 1 teaspoon
Ground cinnamon ½ teaspoon
Grated nutmeg ½ teaspoon

The Café Spice Namasté drunken wet nelly

A classic from Liverpool to which we have added our own twist to make it feel a bit more Indian. The pudding is a bread-and-butter pudding of sorts and made specially as a request by Amanda Callis (a very regular diner) for her step-father's seventieth birthday: we nicknamed it 'Ian Somerville's Drunken Wet Nelly'. In this recipe there is no buttered bread, instead the butter is blended with the sugar. As to why it is named 'wet nelly', please don't ask me, ask a Liverpudlian!

1   Soak the fruit in the port and dark rum for 3–4 hours or overnight.

2   Put the bread cubes in another bowl and pour over the milk. Cover and leave to rest in the fridge for at least 4 hours or overnight.

3   Coat a deep roasting tin or casserole dish with a little oil and line with baking parchment. Preheat the oven to 180°C/350°F/Gas Mark 4.

4   Beat the butter and sugar together until the sugar has dissolved and the butter is pale. Add the eggs one at a time and continue mixing until a smooth batter forms. Add the spices, soaked fruit and bread and mix in gently.

5   Pour into the lined tin or dish and bake for about 10–15 minutes, then turn the oven temperature down to 150°C/300°F/Gas Mark 2 and cook for about 1 hour until soft, but springy to the touch.

6   Cool and serve with some cream or custard.

Serves 10

Mixed dried fruit 500g (1lb 2oz)
Port 100ml (3½fl oz)
Dark rum 50ml (2fl oz)
White bread 1 loaf, crusts discarded and the bread cut into 5cm (2in) squares
Full-fat milk 500ml (18fl oz)
Salted butter 150g (5½oz)
Dark brown sugar 150g (5½oz)
Eggs 4–5, beaten
Ground cardamom 1 teaspoon
Grated nutmeg ¼ teaspoon
Ground cinnamon ½ teaspoon

Simple eggless mango mousse

This is a simple recipe that we used to prepare at the Taj Mahal Hotel in Bombay for the many Indian vegetarians who do not eat egg.

1   Place the cream in a deep bowl, sprinkle the caster sugar over the top, stir gently and refrigerate until ready to whip.

2   Blitz the mango pulp in a blender with the granulated sugar, lime juice and ground cardamom and taste for sweetness and flavour.

3   If using powdered gelatine, you must sprinkle the gelatine over 125ml (4fl oz) water and leave it to rest. Do not stir! If using gelatine sheets, soak in a little cold water until they soften. Leave them both to soak for 30 minutes or so before heating and dissolving.

4   Very gently warm the gelatine until dissolved and mix well. Pour the gelatine into the mango mixture and blitz for a few seconds.

5   Whip the cream to create peaks that will stand.

6   Pour a little mango pulp into the bottom of each glass or bowl. Pour a layer of cream on top, and then layer gently with the mango pulp. Fill a piping bag with the remaining cream, pipe on top of the mango and chill until set.

7   Serve garnished with a few mango slices, some grated lime zest or a sprinkling of chocolate shavings, if you like.

Serves 6

Whipping cream 500ml (18fl oz)
Caster sugar 2 heaped tablespoons
Mango pulp 750ml (1¼ pints),
   (tinned or purée fresh mangoes
   and pass through a sieve)
Granulated sugar 1 tablespoon
Lime juice 1 teaspoon
Ground cardamom ½–1 teaspoon
   (or ground cinnamon)
Vegetarian gelatine powder
   2 tablespoons or 3 sachets
   (check the packet for
   instructions)

To decorate (optional)
Mango slices
Lime zest
Chocolate shavings

Mulberry, walnut, rum & port cake

I use sun-dried Iranian mulberries, which turn a pale colour, rather than the deep purple I would imagine the colour of dried mulberries to be. You can replace these with other dried fruits if you like, as they will all taste great.

1 Soak the mulberries in the port and rum for a minimum of 24 hours, then drain.

2 Line a 23cm (9in) cake tin with baking paper and set aside. Preheat the oven to 130°C/260°F/Gas Mark ¾.

3 Toast the walnuts in the oven for 20 minutes and chop coarsely. Turn up the oven temperature to 160°C/325°F/Gas Mark 3.

4 Sift the flour, baking powder and salt into a large mixing bowl, then stir in the walnuts and set aside.

5 Beat the butter and sugar in a bowl using an electric whisk until smooth and light. Adding one egg to the mixture at a time, beat until well combined. The mixture may look split, but don't worry, it will come back together when the flour is added.

6 Add the flour mixture a little at a time and, using a metal spoon, folding until no lumps remain. Be careful not to overmix or the cake will sink. Mix in the vanilla, rum, mulberries and cardamom.

7 Pour the mixture into the cake tin, level out the top and bake in the middle of the oven for 45 minutes, until golden brown. Turn the cake halfway through the cooking time to ensure an even bake. When the centre is pierced with a thin knife it should come out clean.

8 Cool completely on a wire rack before serving.

Serves 8–10

Dried mulberries 150g (5oz)
Port 150ml (5fl oz)
Dark rum 25ml (1fl oz)
Walnuts 75g (2½oz)
Plain flour 200g (7oz)
Baking powder 1½ teaspoons
Salt ½ teaspoon
Butter 200g (7oz)
Caster sugar 200g (7oz)
Eggs 4
Vanilla extract ½ teaspoon
Ground cardamom ½ teaspoon

Black rice pudding with plums & orange
Suntra ne plum saathe kaara chokha ni kheer

India gave Britain its love for rice pudding. Eaten across the length and breadth of the Indian subcontinent, flavours and styles may differ, but rice, milk and sugar are the three main components that define kheer. I love the flavours of cardamom and saffron and I do not like my kheer too thick, so I tend to keep it a bit more wet than is typical. India grows thousands of varieties of rice and for this recipe I am using glutinous black rice, which has a unique flavour and texture.

1   Rinse the rice to get rid of any powdery residue. Soak in 250ml (9fl oz) of the water and set aside for an hour or two, then drain.

2   Meanwhile, prepare the syrup for the orange and plums. Place the sugar along with the cardamom, lime juice and remaining 600ml (20fl oz) water in a small pan and let soak for a few minutes or until the sugar dissolves. Place over a medium heat and gradually bring to a simmer. Do not stir, but leave a wooden spatula in the syrup and occasionally just move it slightly.

3   Place the orange segments and the plums in two separate frying pans.

4   Simmer the syrup for a few minutes until it thickens, then divide between the two fruit pans. Scrape off any excess. Bring each pan to the boil, then switch off and remove the contents into small bowls.

5   Mix the drained rice with the coconut milk, the 1½ tablespoons of sugar and the cinnamon stick and start to heat over a medium heat. Stir as frequently as you can over a very low heat for 35–40 minutes so the rice gradually releases its starch, plus the cinnamon releases its flavour, and also to avoid the rice sticking at the bottom. High heat will instantly make it stick and you will get a burned rice taste. You may end up needing to add more water or coconut milk.

6   When the rice is cooked, taste to see if you need to add more sugar (bearing in mind that the two fruits are in a syrup), and check the consistency. As the rice cools, it will thicken and set like a jelly, so keep it quite thin.

7   The rice is best served warm along with the two fruits, which can be drizzled over the pudding.

Serves 4–6

Glutinous black rice 200g (7oz) (or other sticky rice)
Water 850ml (1½ pints)
Caster sugar 500g (1lb 2 oz), plus 1½ tablespoons for the rice
Green cardamom pods 3, seeds roughly crushed
Lime juice from 1 lime
Oranges 2–3, peeled and segmented
Plums 6–8, cut into pieces
Coconut milk 600ml (20fl oz)
Cinnamon stick 5cm (2in) piece

Note
For an added crunch, serve this with lightly toasted coconut chips or toasted nuts.

Steamed cabinet pudding our-style

There was a time in Bombay's many bakery cafés or, as we called them, 'Irani restaurants', when most steamed puddings seemed to be made using leftover bread or cake pieces with diced dried fruit (tutti-frutti) and served up as cabinet puddings. They are actually quite delicious when eaten with double cream or a vanilla-and-nutmeg custard sauce and some seasonal fresh berries.

1 Liberally butter six or so small ovenproof dishes or bowls. Sprinkle over some flour and rotate the mould so that it is well coated. If there are any gaps, apply more butter and dust again with flour. Chill until needed.

2 Sift the flour, cardamom and baking powder into a mixing bowl and stir in the cake crumbs and the dried peel and fruit. Mix well so that the dried fruit is coated with flour.

3 In another mixing bowl, use a hand mixer to beat the butter and sugar until light and fluffy.

4 Place a deep baking tray filled with 1cm (½in) of boiling water on the middle shelf of the oven, and preheat to 150°C/300°F/Gas Mark 2.

5 Mix the eggs into the butter mixture. It may look curdled at this stage, but that is fine. Add the vanilla.

6 Using a metal spoon, fold the flour and fruit mixture into the eggs and butter and mix well. Pour the mixture into the chilled moulds.

7 Carefully place the moulds in the baking tray filled with the water and bake for 20–25 minutes or until done. Check with a knife or skewer to see if it comes out clean.

8 Turn out and serve warm with cream or custard and some fresh berries.

Serves 6–8

Salted butter 150g (5½oz), plus extra for the dish
Plain flour 150g (5½oz), plus extra for the dish
Green cardamom pods 1 teaspoon, seeds ground
Baking powder 1½ teaspoons
Cake crumbs 150g (5½oz) (use any dry, un-iced cake pieces and blitz in a blender)
Mixed chopped peel 150g (5½oz)
Sultanas or raisins 100g (3½oz)
Caster sugar 200g (7oz)
Eggs 4, beaten
Vanilla extract 1 teaspoon

Notes
Do not throw away any leftover stale cake. Simply dry in the oven and store in a jar until needed.

You can make these in advance: just reheat in the oven with water, but this time keep the mould covered.

White marrow halva
Dodhi no halwo

India has several varieties of squashes and marrows and this recipe is adaptable to them all. The moisture content in each variety differs and that will affect the cooking times and colour, but you are guaranteed a great taste. A 'halwa', or as we Parsees and Gujaratis say a 'halwo', is quite simply a fudge.

1   Take a deep pan, wok or a kadhai and heat the ghee over a medium heat. Place a sieve over a mixing bowl.

2   When the ghee is reasonably hot, add the sultanas and nuts and fry until the cashew nuts just start to change colour.

3   Immediately strain over the bowl and, with a piece of kitchen paper, wipe out the pan and place it back on the heat. Toss the contents of the sieve a couple of times, as the remaining heat can continue to cook and brown the nuts, making them bitter.

4   Add the strained ghee back into the pan and reheat. Add the crushed cardamom pods and, after a few seconds, the grated marrow or squash and stir continuously to prevent it from sticking. Cook until the water from the vegetable has completely cooked off.

5   Add the evaporated milk and, using a flat wooden spatula, stir regularly as the milk solids will stick to the bottom of the pan. Once the milk is reduced by more than half, about 10–15 minutes, add the sugar and continue cooking and stirring until the mixture is thick and starts coming off the sides of the pan and the fat starts to be released.

6   Pour the thickened fudge into a flat dish or baking tray and flatten the surface. Sprinkle over the fried nuts and sultanas and press down slightly. Cut into small squares to serve.

7   Serve warm or cold with ice cream or fresh cream.

Makes 20 pieces

Ghee 5–6 tablespoons
Sultanas 1–2 tablespoons
Unskinned almonds 8–10, chopped
Pistachios 12–15, chopped
Cashew nuts 8–10, chopped
Green cardamom pods 5–6, cracked open
Marrow, squash or gourd 500g (1lb 2oz) peeled, deseeded and thickly grated (grated weight)
Evaporated milk 500–600ml (18–20fl oz)
Caster sugar 5–6 tablespoons

Note
Taste the marrow, squash or gourd before grating and, if it is bitter, then use another one.

Hazelnut kulfi
Hejhalanata kulfi

Kulfi is often known as an Indian-style ice cream, but I prefer to call kulfis 'iced cream' because they are simply frozen after the initial prep, without any stirring or beating. Traditionally, the milk would be gradually reduced over a slow heat to reduce the water content and prevent ice crystals from forming when freezing. However, I thought it would be easier to bypass that tedious stage and give you something very simple and easy to work with. Toasted hazelnuts or almonds can be used instead of pistachios. Traditionally kulfi is served alongside rose-scented rice or agar-agar vermicelli and soaked basil seeds, but you can serve it as you desire, perhaps with some diced fresh fruit. A typical kulfi mould is conical shaped, but use any small pudding mould or ice cream mould for this.

1   Preheat the oven to 130°C/260°F/Gas Mark ¾.

2   Place the hazelnuts on a baking tray and toast in the oven for 20–25 minutes. Remove from the oven and let cool completely.

3   Place the milk in a saucepan over a low heat, until just warm.

4   Transfer most of the hazelnuts to a blender and pour over the warmed milk. Soak for about 30 minutes, then blend to a paste.

5   Add the cream to the hazelnut mixture, and then, tasting as you go and adding a little bit at a time, mix in the condensed milk and ground cardamom. The cardamom shouldn't cancel out the flavour of the hazelnut and the sweetness can be adjusted with the addition of the condensed milk.

6   Place the bowl in the freezer for 20–30 minutes or until the mixture has thickened slightly.

7   Chop the remaining nuts and add these to the mixture, saving a sprinkling to serve. Pour the mixture into the moulds and return to the freezer until completely frozen. If making lollies, you can insert the sticks halfway through the freezing.

8   To serve, briefly dip the moulds into hot water and then turn out on a serving plate. Serve immediately, with the reserved chopped nuts sprinkled on top.

Serves 6–8

Skinned hazelnuts 200–250g (7–9oz)
Full-fat milk 250ml (9fl oz)
Double cream 500ml (18fl oz)
Condensed milk 300ml (10fl oz)
Green cardamom pods
½ teaspoon, seeds ground

Note
Kulfi is not an ice cream and will take longer than ice cream to melt and soften.

9

EXTRAS

*

Tomato, onion & cucumber salad
Good ol' cachumber

This simple onion salad is a must when we eat a biryani, a mixed pilau with raita or a curry and rice. Pictured opposite.

1   If the onion is quite strong, place in a colander and rinse under cold water. Break up all the pieces.

2   In a serving bowl, mix together all of the ingredients apart from the ground cumin. Sprinkle over the cumin before serving.

Serves 4–5

Red onions 2, finely chopped
Fresh green chillies 2–3, finely chopped
Fresh coriander sprigs 8–9, leaves finely chopped
Fresh mint 20–30 leaves, shredded
Plum tomatoes 1–2, pulp removed and flesh diced
Cucumber ½ large or 1 small, cored and finely chopped
Lime juice or cider vinegar 1 tablespoon
Salt ½ teaspoon
Ground cumin 1 teaspoon, toasted, to sprinkle

Yogurt & mint sauce
Dahi pudina sauce

This is one of the most popular sauces in India as it goes with so many different meals and snacks.

1   Place the yogurt, mint, lime juice, sugar and half the cumin in a blender. Blitz together until the yogurt is smooth and the mint is almost puréed. Taste and add a salt if necessary.

2   Place in a serving bowl and top with a dusting of the remaining cumin and the chilli powder.

Serves 10

Thick Greek yogurt 200ml (7fl oz)
Fresh mint 25–30 leaves, chopped
Lime juice 1 teaspoon
Sugar 1 teaspoon
Cumin seeds 2 teaspoons, toasted and finely crushed
Salt
Red chilli powder 1 teaspoon

Fresh green chutney with roasted yellow split peas
Channa ni daal nay sing ni leeli chutney

This is lovely in sandwiches and as a dip for snacks. Pictured opposite, right.

1   Rinse the yellow split peas and soak in warm water for 3–4 hours. Add some oil to a frying pan over a low heat, drain the peas and add to the pan. Sauté until dried out and slightly bruised with brown marks, about 5–10 minutes. Set aside to cool.

2   Place all of the ingredients in a blender and purée for a thick, yet smooth texture. Add a little more water if needed. Stop halfway and scrape down the sides. Taste and add a bit more lime juice if preferred.

3   This is a fresh chutney and will not keep for very long, so eat and enjoy.

Makes 2 x 250g (9oz) jars

Yellow split peas (channa daal)
   1½ tablespoons
Oil
Fresh coriander 1 bunch, stalks
   and leaves roughly chopped
Fresh mint 30–40 leaves
Fresh ginger 5–7.5cm (2–3in) piece,
   peeled and chopped
Garlic 2–3 cloves
Lime juice from 1 lime
Fresh green chillies 3–4
Cumin seeds ½ teaspoon
Sugar 2–3 teaspoons
Roasted peanuts 1–2 tablespoons
Water 200ml (7fl oz)
Salt

Preserved mango chutney with ginger & cumin
Aadu murcha jeeru nay khaan ma kaeri

This easy chutney will outclass any ready-made one. Pictured opposite, middle.

1   Place the sugar, vinegar, cinnamon and salt in a casserole dish and heat gently until the sugar dissolves and starts to heat through. Do not boil.

2   In a dry frying pan, gently toast the cumin, cardamom and the dried red chillies until crisp and aromatic. Let cool. Add the toasted spices to a small blender along with the ginger and blitz to a fine paste.

3   Stir this paste into the sugar solution. Stirring regularly, heat until it comes to the boil, then add the mango. Bring it to a gently rolling boil and cook for roughly 20–30 minutes until you get the consistency of jam. Remove and discard the cinnamon. Spoon into sterilized jars (see page 180).

4   The chutney will keep for up to a year unopened, but once opened, keep in the fridge and use within a month.

Makes 2 x 500g (1lb 2 oz) jars

Soft dark brown sugar 250g (9oz)
Cider vinegar 250ml (9fl oz)
Cinnamon stick 2.5–5cm (1–2in)
Sea salt 2 teaspoons
Cumin seeds 1 teaspoon
Green cardamom pods 8–10,
   cracked open
Dried red chillies 4–6 largish types
Fresh ginger 7.5cm (3in) piece,
   peeled and chopped
Semi-ripe to ripe mangoes
   7–8, peeled and flesh diced

Hot red chutney
Tikhi laal chutney

This is a versatile chutney, for when you want to add a bit of oomph to your dish. Blend with some tomato ketchup to give it an extra twist. Adding oil will preserve the chutney so that you can keep in the fridge for 3–4 weeks. Pictured on previous page, left.

1   Heat a non-stick frying pan over a medium heat. Add the yellow split peas and keep pan-roasting them until they brown a little and, when bitten, are almost brittle.

2   Break the red chillies into pieces and set aside. Do not discard the seeds, just the stems.

3   Add the onion, ginger and garlic to the pan of split peas and cook until just roasted, about 4–5 minutes.

4   Add the split peas, chillies, onion, ginger, garlic and salt to a blender along with a little water and purée to a fine paste. Add more water as needed. If you like, add some oil and blend again – the oil will act as a preservative and will prevent the chutney from drying out.

5   Store the chutney in the sterilized jar for up to 3–4 weeks.

Makes 1 x 250g (9oz) jar

Yellow split peas (channa daal)
   2–3 tablespoons
Mixed dried red chillies 6–7 (large and small)
Red onion 1 small, diced
Fresh ginger 2.5–5cm (1–2in) piece, peeled
   and chopped
Garlic 6–8 cloves, cut into small pieces
Salt ½ teaspoon
Oil 2–3 tablespoons (optional)

Note
To sterilize the jar, first preheat your oven to 140°C/275°F/Gas Mark 1. Wash the jar well and place the jar and lid in the oven for 5–10 minutes. Turn the oven down to 100°C/200°F/Gas Mark ¼ and keep the jar hot until it is ready to fill.
   When ready, use oven gloves to remove the jar from the oven, and fill. Seal immediately and let cool. Immerse the jar in a bowl filled with ice and water to create a good seal.

Simple lime, lemon & chilli pickle
Limbu, marcha nu achaar

This pickle takes little time to prepare, but demands patience to abstain from wanting to eat it too soon. Most Indian pickles are made with mustard oil, and Britain produces excellent versions. But if you cannot find mustard oil, don't worry, just use extra-virgin cold-pressed rapeseed oil. Pictured overleaf, middle.

1   Dice the limes and lemons into 1cm (½in) pieces, discarding any seeds. Place the lime, lemon and chilli in a glass or steel bowl and mix them with the turmeric and salt. Cover the bowl and leave it aside for 2–3 days. If possible, mix once or twice a day, clean the edges with kitchen paper and cover.

2   Strain and pour any water collected from the marinating mixture into a saucepan.

3   Add the water, sugar and the vinegar to the pan and gradually bring to the boil over a medium heat. Let simmer for 15 minutes until thickened like a syrup. Keep warm.

4   Heat the oil in a casserole dish large enough to hold all the other ingredients and cook the mustard seeds over a medium heat for a minute until fragrant, but do not let burn. Add the cumin and coriander seeds and sauté for 30 seconds, then add the ginger and garlic.

5   Sauté until the garlic changes colour, about 2 minutes, then add the red chilli powder.

6   As soon as the powder has been absorbed, add the lime and lemon mixture and sauté for 4–5 minutes until any liquid evaporates. Add the syrup and bring back to the boil. Cook for a minute or so, then remove from the heat.

7   Transfer to sterilized jars (see opposite), seal and set aside for 2–3 weeks, then enjoy. The pickle will last for up to a year in the fridge. The oil that will be created can be used as a seasoning for cooked rice or drizzled over dishes once the pickle is finished.

Makes 2 x 250g (9oz) jars

Unwaxed limes 5–6
Unwaxed lemons 4–5
Fresh green chillies 8–10,
  cut into 1cm (½in) slices
Ground turmeric 3 teaspoons
Sea salt 2–3 tablespoons
Water 200ml (7fl oz)
Sugar 200g (7oz)
White wine vinegar
  4–5 tablespoons
Mustard oil 200ml (7fl oz)
Black mustard seeds 1 heaped
  tablespoon, crushed
Cumin seeds 3 teaspoons, crushed
Coriander seeds 5 heaped
  tablespoons, crushed
Fresh ginger 10cm (4in) piece,
  peeled and finely chopped
Garlic 6–8 cloves, finely chopped
Red chilli powder 1 teaspoon

Beetroot & mustard water pickle
Chukundar kaa paniwala achaar

This is really simple to make and keeps extremely well. Just let it ferment well. This can be made with any beetroot, but the red is most alluring. Pictured opposite, left.

1   Mix all of the ingredients together in a glass mixing bowl and cover loosely with a cloth for 10–12 days. Keep it on the worktop and mix daily, wiping the sides clean with kitchen paper.

2   Transfer to sterilized jars (see page 180) and then refrigerate. This will keep for up to 6 months.

Makes 2 x 500g (1lb 2oz) jars

Raw beetroot 6 small, chopped
Fresh green chillies 10 finger-type, shredded
Fresh ginger 150g (5½oz), piece peeled and sliced
Thin spring onions 8, sliced
Sugar 4 tablespoons
English mustard 4 tablespoons
Lime juice 5 tablespoons
Cumin seeds 1 tablespoon
Coriander seeds 3 tablespoons, crushed
Cider vinegar 6 tablespoons
Salt 3 tablespoons

Mixed peppers in yogurt

This is a surprising condiment that works well with so many different dishes. I always keep a jar of this in my fridge. Pictured opposite, right.

1   Toast the mustard seeds, fennel seeds and coriander seeds in a dry frying pan over a medium heat until aromatic, then crush coarsely.

2   Mix the yogurt with the turmeric, jaggery, salt and oil until the jaggery is completely dissolved. Add all the other ingredients and mix everything together well.

3   Place in a small stainless steel or glass container, cover loosely with a cloth. Keep on the worktop and mix daily for a couple of days. Place in sterilized jars (see page 180) and refrigerate for up to 6 months.

Makes 3 x 250g (9oz) jars

Mustard seeds 2 tablespoons
Fennel seeds 2 tablespoons
Coriander seeds 1 tablespoon
Yogurt 3 tablespoons
Ground turmeric 1 teaspoon
Jaggery, dark brown or muscovado sugar 50g (1¾oz)
Salt 2 tablespoons
Oil 150ml (5fl oz)
Green peppers 2, sliced lengthways
Mini mixed peppers 10, sliced
Fresh green chillies 15, chopped

Garlic & peanut pickle
Lasooni shingdanay achaar

An easy-to-make garlic and peanut pickle that will keep refrigerated for up to 5 months if it is stored carefully. Add a bit more oil and it will keep for even longer. Garlic has long been pickled in India and several types exist, with some very much trademarks of certain communities. This can be enjoyed with daal, curries and rice. This is quite a hot pickle, but since it is a condiment it can just be used sparingly.

1   Preheat the oven to 140°C/275°F/Gas Mark 1.

2   Gently toast the masala spices by placing all the ingredients on a small baking tray and cooking in the oven for 10–12 minutes, then switch the oven off and leave inside for another 30 minutes. Grind to a fine powder in a small blender or crush as finely as possible in a mortar.

3   Heat the oil in a wok, a kadhai or a casserole dish over a medium–high heat. Turn the heat down and add the green chillies, if using, the garlic and peanuts and as soon the garlic or peanuts change colour ever so slightly, add the turmeric and continue sautéing over a low heat for 2–3 minutes, stirring continuously.

4   Add the lime juice and continue stirring for 2–3 minutes until the garlic and peanuts have softened. Add the red chilli powder and the jaggery or soft brown sugar and keep stirring until the sugar has dissolved.

5   Stir in the powdered masala and salt and cook for another minute or so.

6   Remove from the heat and let cool. Transfer to sterilized jars (see page 180) and wait at least a week before using. If you add some more oil, it will keep for months in the fridge.

Makes 2 x 250g (9oz) jars

Mustard oil 5 tablespoons (or extra-virgin rapeseed oil)
Fresh green chillies 4–6, cut into 1cm (½in) pieces (optional)
Garlic 200g (7oz) cloves, peeled and chopped
Skinned peanuts 200g (7oz), coarsely chopped and shaken in a sieve to get rid of any powder
Ground turmeric 1 level teaspoon
Lime juice 3–4 tablespoons
Red chilli powder 2 tablespoons
Jaggery, soft brown or raw cane sugar 1½ heaped tablespoons
Salt 1 heaped teaspoon

For the masala
Mustard seeds 3 teaspoons
Cumin seeds 1 heaped teaspoon
Coriander seeds 1 tablespoon
Asafoetida ½ teaspoon (optional)

Tomato & garlic mayonnaise

This mayonnaise works very well with fried foods such as fritters and chips, and as a dip for canapés. I often make tartare sauce with this mayo by adding chopped capers, gherkins and parsley.

1   Add all the ingredients except for the oil and the ketchup to a food processor and blitz for 30 seconds.

2   Gradually pour the oil into the food processer in a steady stream – hold at an angle to prevent the oil from splashing.

3   The mayonnaise will thicken as the oil is added, and as it reaches a point where there is no movement, stop the machine and slightly shake to release any trapped air. Do this a couple of times to create an amazingly thick mayonnaise. Add the ketchup and give it another blitz, then check the consistency, adding more oil if too thin.

4   Check the seasoning and transfer to sterilized jars (see page 180). Store in the fridge until needed.

Makes 2 x 500g (1lb 2oz) jars

Eggs 2
Worcestershire sauce 2 teaspoons
Lime juice from 1 lime
Sugar 1 tablespoon
Hot English mustard 1 tablespoon
Garlic 3–4 cloves
Fresh green chillies 3–4, chopped
Fresh coriander 4–5 sprigs
Salt 1–2 teaspoons
Groundnut oil 750ml–1 litre
   (1¼–1¾ pints)
Tomato ketchup 4–5 tablespoons

Spiced tomato ketchup

You can make this into a creamier sauce by adding a tablespoon of mayonnaise. This is delicious served with an omelette.

1   Mix together all of the ingredients, apart from the Tabasco. Add Tabasco to taste. Place in a small bowl and serve with whatever you fancy.

Makes 1 small jar

Tomato ketchup 1–2 tablespoons
Fresh green chillies 1–2, finely
   chopped
English mustard 1 teaspoon
Tabasco, to taste

Fermented cabbage & carrot with cumin
Deshi kimchee

Kimchee or kimchi has become increasingly popular due to its positive impact on digestion. It is also delicious when paired with any spicy or hot foods as the spices will add glamour to your plate. Pictured opposite.

1   Mix all of the ingredients together and cover loosely with a cloth for 10 days. Keep on the worktop and mix daily, wiping the sides clean with a piece of kitchen paper.

2   Transfer to sterilized jars (see page 180) and then refrigerate. It will keep for 1–2 weeks.

Makes 3 x 250g (9oz) jars

Cabbage 300g, shredded
Carrots 2, shredded
Fresh ginger 7.5cm (3in) piece, peeled and finely chopped
Garlic 5 cloves, finely chopped
Fresh green chillies 6–8 finger-type, finely chopped
Red onions 2, finely chopped
Cumin seeds 1 tablespoon, crushed
Salt 2 tablespoons
Fresh curry leaves 25–30, shredded; if using dried, soak in water for 10–12 minutes, and dry thoroughly before shredding
Red chilli powder 1½ tablespoons
Lime juice 4 tablespoons

Garam masala

This spice mix is made from ingredients included in the Spice Box and is a great addition to a variety of dishes.

1   Preheat the oven to 130°C/260°F/Gas Mark ¾. Place all the spices on a baking tray, place on the middle shelf of the oven and bake for 10–12 minutes.

2   Turn off the oven, leaving the tray inside for another 20 minutes. Remove the spices from the tray and let cool completely.

3   Transfer the spice mixture to a blender and blitz to a fine powder. Store in an airtight container for 2–3 months. Best kept in the fridge or in a cool dark place.

Makes 1 x 250g (9oz) jar

Cardamom pods 6–8, seeds crushed
Cinnamon stick 2 x 7.5cm (3in) pieces
Cumin seeds 1 tablespoon
Coriander seeds 2 tablespoons
Black peppercorns 1 teaspoon

Ginger & garlic paste
Adoo lasan

This is a very useful paste, as garlic and ginger are so often used in Indian recipes. The important thing is to work with equal weights of ginger and garlic, whatever amount you want to make. Those listed below are just examples. The larger your blender, the more you will need in order for the blades to process it efficiently.

1 Put the garlic and ginger into a blender, add the oil and a dash of water and blitz to a purée. If too thick, add more water and a little more oil until smooth in consistency.

2 Transfer to a sterilized jar (see page 130), cover with a layer of oil to preserve, seal tightly and store in the fridge for up to 3 months. Use as needed, always using a dry spoon and keeping the rim of the container clean. If the paste begins to dry out, pour some more oil over the top before resealing.

Makes 1 x 250g (9oz) jar

Garlic 115g (4oz) cloves, roughly chopped
Fresh ginger 115g (4oz), peeled and roughly chopped
Oil (any except olive oil) about 2 tablespoons, plus extra for preserving

Green coconut chutney
Leeli nariyal ni chutney

This is wonderfully fragrant and perfect for cooling down very hot curries.

1 Drain the desiccated coconut, discarding the water and placing the coconut flesh in a blender. Add the coriander, mint, chilli, garlic, cumin, sugar and half the lime juice. Blitz until it is a thick paste, adding a little water if the mixture needs loosening.

2 Taste and season with a little salt, adding more lime juice if you like.

Makes 1 x 250g (9oz) jar

Desiccated coconut 150g (5oz), soaked in warm water for 30 minutes
Fresh coriander a large handful
Fresh mint a large handful
Fresh green chillies 4–5
Garlic 6–8 cloves
Cumin seeds 1 heaped teaspoon
Sugar 1 tablespoon
Lime juice from 1 lime
Salt

Thrashed red chilli & cumin seasoning
Laal mirich aur jeera masala

This works very well with salads. I recommend trying it on fried eggs too...

1   Preheat the oven to 140°C/275°F/Gas Mark 1. Line a baking tray with a silicon mat or baking parchment.

2   Blitz all of the ingredients in a food processor.

3   Spread the mixture out on the prepared baking sheet.

4   Roast in the centre of the oven for 5–6 minutes, then remove and stir gently with a spatula, checking if it has become sticky. If the sugar is still intact, return to the oven for another 2–3 minutes and check again.

5   Remove and let cool. It will solidify as it cools. When cold, break it into chunks with your hands and place in a sterilized jar (see page 180).

6   This will last for up to 6 months in the fridge and can be used on top of salads and fried eggs.

Makes 1 x 250g (9oz) jar

Crushed red chillies 2 tablespoons
Cumin seeds 1 teaspoon, well crushed
Sugar 4 tablespoons
Salt 1 tablespoon

Jeeravan masala

This is a tangy yet hot and spicy masala used as a taste enhancer. It is mostly used as a seasoning to give snack foods that extra oomph. In the summer, it is also sprinkled over fresh fruit salads, which may sound strange but do try it – you will be hooked.

1   Heat the oven to 150°C/300°F/Gas Mark 2. Put all the ingredients on a baking tray and mix them together. Place the tray in the middle of the oven for 10 minutes, then switch off the oven and leave in there for an hour or so.

2   Remove and let cool until crisp. Grind all the spices together to a powder and place in an airtight container. Keep in the fridge or a cool dark place.

Makes 1 x 250g (9oz) jar

Cumin seeds 3 teaspoons
Coriander seeds 2 teaspoons
Bay leaves 3–4
Dried red chillies 6–8 large
Salt 1 teaspoon
Fennel seeds 2 teaspoons
Ground turmeric ½ teaspoon
Ground cinnamon ½ teaspoon
Cardamom pods 1–2, crushed
Salt ¾ teaspoon
Grated nutmeg a pinch

Channa masala

This is a very useful spice mix to keep in your spice drawer. I have used it in multiple recipes in the book and it works well not just with chickpeas, but also other peas, pulses and whole lentils. Pictured opposite.

1   Preheat the oven to 150°C/300°F/Gas Mark 2.

2   Mix all of the ingredients together and spread out on a small baking tray. Roast for 10 minutes, then switch off the oven and leave inside for another 15–20 minutes. Cool and grind to a fine powder. Store in an airtight container for 2–3 months. Keep in the fridge if you have space, or a cool dark place.

Makes 1 small jar

Cinnamon stick 2.5cm (1in) piece
Black cardamom pods 2, cracked
   open
Black peppercorns 4–5
Cloves 2–3
Bay leaves 2–3
Fennel seeds 1 teaspoon
Cumin seeds 1 teaspoon
Coriander seeds 1 teaspoon
Dried pomegranate seeds
   1 teaspoon
Dried red chillies 2–3, deseeded
   and stems removed

Paneer

Fresh paneer is really easy to make and it is wonderfully soft and creamy. Once separated, do not throw away the whey as it can be used to make bread, or it is delicious when seasoned and served cold as a drink.

1   Line a colander with a muslin cloth or clean tea towel and place a bowl underneath to collect the whey.

2   Add the milk to a saucepan and place over a medium–high heat. Once the milk is boiling, add the yogurt and stir. Continue to stir the mixture until the milk has curdled and split well.

3   Once curdled, take the pan off the heat and immediately pour it through the lined colander. Remove the bowl of whey and rinse the solids under cold running water to stop the curdling process. Drain, squeeze and hang the solids for at least 30 minutes. The paneer should be soft but well-drained.

Makes 1 block

Full-fat milk 1½ litres (50fl oz)
Live yogurt 150ml (5fl oz)

Spicy tomato sauce

This sauce can be used with many dishes and works really well when paired with the marrow koftas on page 96.

1   Mix the ground coriander, chilli powder and turmeric in a small bowl with 3–4 tablespoons of cold water and stir to make a paste. Cover and set aside.

2   Heat the ghee or oil in a large, heavy-based pan over a medium heat and add the cardamom pods, cloves, cinnamon and bay leaves and stir-fry for about a minute, or until the cardamom pods start to change colour and the cloves swell. Add the onion and, while stirring with a wooden spatula, sauté until pale in colour, about 3–4 minutes.

3   Add the ginger & garlic paste and cook for 2–3 minutes. Add the spice paste and season with a little salt. Add a little more water to the paste bowl, stirring to mix in any remaining spices and add to the pan.

4   Continue cooking for 2–3 minutes, or until the moisture has evaporated. When the bubbles in the pan start to show oil, the masala is cooked.

5   Add the puréed tomatoes to the pan and cook for another 5 minutes, or until specks of oil begin to reappear on the surface. Pour in the water and bring to the boil. Reduce the heat to low and let simmer, stirring frequently, for 2–3 minutes. Adjust the seasoning and garnish with chopped coriander to serve.

Makes 1 jar

Ground coriander 1 tablespoon
Red chilli powder 1 teaspoon
Ground turmeric ½ teaspoon
Ghee 2 heaped tablespoons **or oil** 3 tablespoons
Green cardamom pods 3, crushed
Garlic 2 cloves
Cinnamon stick 3–6cm (1¼–2½in) piece
Bay leaves 2
Onions 2 small, finely chopped
Ginger & garlic paste (see page 188), 2 tablespoons
Salt
Tomatoes 6, puréed, or use a 400g (14 oz) tin
Water 250ml (9fl oz)
Coriander leaves, chopped, to garnish

Sizzled lentils with garlic, cumin & chilli
Tarka daal

This is a great basic recipe, but feel free to add any other spices or extras that you like. For example, you could include more garlic or chilli, or some ground coriander or dried red chillies instead of fresh green chillies, or even some finely sliced ginger.

1 Place the lentils in a sieve and thoroughly rinse under cold running water. Add the lentils to a saucepan and cover with enough cold water to come 2.5cm (1in) above the lentils. Bring to a boil. Skim off any froth that appears. Once the water has come to a simmer, add the turmeric and half the butter. Simmer gently for about 20 minutes, or until the lentils are soft and the water has been absorbed.

2 In the meantime, heat a dry frying pan over a medium heat. Add the cumin seeds and fry for a couple of minutes until toasted and aromatic. Remove the seeds from the pan and set aside. Add the remaining butter to the pan and, once melted, fry the garlic and chilli for 1–2 minutes, or until the garlic turns a light golden-brown and the chilli is softened. Add the toasted cumin seeds back into the pan and remove from the heat.

3 Give the lentils a stir to break them up and add the chilli and garlic. Mix well. Taste and adjust the seasoning.

Serves 4

Red lentils 400g (14oz)
Ground turmeric 2 teaspoons
Butter 25g (1oz)
Cumin seeds 3 teaspoons
Garlic 4 cloves, finely chopped
Fresh green chillies 2–3, finely chopped
Salt and freshly ground black pepper

Hot madras curry powder

Most traditional kitchens would not use this, but as it works in many recipes and is hugely popular across the UK, I thought that it would be a useful addition.

1 Preheat the oven to 160°C/325°F/Gas Mark 3.

2 Place the red chillies on one baking tray and the rest of the ingredients on the second. Place in the oven and roast for 10 minutes. Turn off the oven and leave in the switched off oven for 15–20 minutes.

3 Grind the chillies to a fine powder, then grind the other ingredients. Sift everything through a fine sieve. Grind any larger pieces and sift again.

4 Store in an airtight container for 10–12 months. Keep in the fridge or a cool dark place.

Makes 1 small jar

Dried red chillies 50g (1¾oz)
Coriander seeds 80g (2¾oz)
Cumin seeds 1 tablespoon
Black mustard seeds ½ teaspoon
Black peppercorns 8–10
Asafoetida, a pinch (optional)
Ground turmeric ¾ teaspoon
Fresh curry leaves 8–10, shredded; if using dried, soak in water for 10–12 minutes, and dry thoroughly before shredding
Split yellow peas 150g (5¼oz)

Keralan-style seasoned buttermilk
Moru

Several hundred buttermilk recipes abound across India. More so because traditional buttermilk was generated in the house almost daily when raw milk was heated, then had to be left outside due to a lack of refrigeration. This led to the production of raw cheese (paneer), with buttermilk as a by-product. To combat its acidic nature, several different styles of tempering spices are added across India. Here is a simple one. This can be served as a warm drink, but more usually forms the 'curry' element for soaking into rice. Serve with rice, fried papads (poppadums), some chutney or pickle, or with a vegetable fritter or fried snack.

1   Heat the oil in a deep saucepan over a medium heat until hot but not smoking. Add the mustard seeds and reduce the heat slightly. As soon as the spluttering settles, add the cumin seeds, red chillies and curry leaves.

2   Sauté for a few seconds until the chillies change colour, then add the ginger, garlic and green chillies. As the garlic changes colour, add the shallots and sauté, mixing well until the shallots change colour to a pale brown, about 6 minutes.

3   Add the turmeric and mix in well, then in a few seconds turn the heat off. Stir in the buttermilk, season and mix well.

4   Return to a medium heat and bring to just below boiling. Do not let boil, just keep hot. Serve with some rice.

Serves 4–6

Coconut oil 2 tablespoons
Black mustard seeds 1 heaped teaspoon
Cumin seeds 1 teaspoon
Dried red chillies 3–4 large, broken into pieces and deseeded
Curry leaves 12–15, preferably fresh, shredded; if using dried, soak in water for 10–12 minutes, and dry thoroughly before shredding
Fresh ginger 5cm (2in) piece, peeled and finely chopped
Garlic 4–5 cloves, finely chopped
Fresh green chillies 3–4 finger-type, slit down the middle
Shallots 5–6, thinly sliced
Ground turmeric ½ teaspoon
Buttermilk 500ml (18fl oz)
Salt

Note
The chillies can be removed after cooking and the sauce puréed. Add them back in if you are serving with rice or serve without, warm, as a nourishing drink to accompany your meal.

Lentil pilau
Masoor daal khichdi

This is a great accompaniment to so many of the recipes in this book and is a simple recipe that you will use time and time again. You can also simply enjoy this with a couple of dollops of Greek yogurt.

1   Preheat the oven to 140°C/275°F/Gas Mark 1.

2   Heat the oil in a large casserole dish over a medium heat. When hot, add the cardamom pods and bay leaf and sauté for about 1 minute.

3   Add the shallots and garlic and cook very gently for 2–3 minutes, without letting the shallots colour, and stirring occasionally. Pour in the measured water or stock, add a little salt and mix well.

4   Bring back to the boil and add the rice and lentils. Let cook for 5–6 minutes, stirring regularly. Once most of the water has been absorbed, cover the dish and place in the oven for 10 minutes. Turn off the heat and leave in the oven for another 10 minutes.

5   When ready, season the mixture with pepper. Fold in the butter, stirring until it has all melted. Remove the whole spices if you wish, and serve.

Serves 4–5

Extra-virgin rapeseed oil
   1 tablespoon
Green cardamom pods 3, crushed
Bay leaf 1
Shallots 2, finely chopped
Garlic 1–2 cloves, chopped
Boiling water or vegetable stock
   750–900ml (1⅓–1½ pints)
Basmati rice 350g (12oz), washed
   and drained
**Pink lentils (masoor daal) or split
   mung beans (mung daal)**
   100–150g (3½–5oz), soaked in
   water for 1–2 hours and drained
Butter 30g (1oz)
**Salt and freshly ground black
   pepper**

Fragrant rice

This method will give you delicious, fluffy rice every time.

1   Preheat the oven to 140°C/275°F/Gas Mark 1.

2   Heat the oil in a large casserole dish over a medium heat. When hot, add the whole spices and sauté for about 1 minute.

3   Add the shallots and cook very gently for 2–3 minutes, without letting them colour. Stir occasionally. Pour in the water, mix well and bring back to the boil. Add the rice and cook, while stirring, until about half of the liquid is absorbed.

4   Half cover the dish and place in the oven for 20 minutes. Remove from the oven, fluff with a fork and serve.

Serves 4

Extra-virgin rapeseed oil
   1 tablespoon
Cinnamon stick 1 x 6cm
   (2½in) piece **or cardamom pods**
   2 **or cumin seeds** ½ teaspoon
Shallots 2, finely sliced
Boiling water 700ml (1¼ pints)
Basmati rice 350g (12oz), washed
   and drained

Spiced pepper rice

Rice dishes are a staple in Indian cooking, and on a table laden with food there will always be at least one rice dish. This is a really tasty and straightforward recipe that will pair well with curries, lentils and other sides.

1   Preheat the oven to 150°C/300°F/Gas Mark 2.

2   Place a large ovenproof saucepan over a medium heat. Once hot, add the oil and the cardamom pods. Fry until the cardamoms change colour, about 2 minutes. Add the red chilli and fry for another minute. Then add the garlic and fry for 1 minute, stirring frequently. As soon as the garlic changes colour to a light golden brown, add the onion and keep stirring. Cook until the onion turns a light golden brown, about 4–5 minutes.

3   Stir in the peppers and fry for further 2 minutes. Add the stock to the pan, bring back to the boil, add the rice and return to the boil again.

4   Cover the pan and place it in the oven for 20 minutes or until all the liquid has been absorbed. Remove from the oven and stir in the tomatoes. Season with salt and pepper and serve immediately.

Serves 4

Sunflower oil 2 tablespoons
Cardamom pods 3, crushed
Fresh red chilli 1, finely chopped
Garlic 6 cloves, finely chopped
Onion 1, finely sliced
Green pepper 1, diced
Red pepper 1, diced
Vegetable stock 700ml (1¼ pints)
Basmati rice 350g (12oz), washed and drained
Plum tomatoes 2, seeds removed and flesh diced
Salt and freshly ground black pepper

Chapattis

If you have some time, then I really recommend that you make these from scratch. There is nothing quite like making and enjoying them fresh. Engage with your artistic talents and see how often you can actually shape them as round!

1 Sift the flour and salt into a large bowl. Make a well in the centre and pour in the warm oil. Add just a little of the water and mix together, adding more water a little at a time and kneading between additions until a dough forms. You may not need to use all of the water.

2 Continue kneading for 3–4 minutes, until the dough comes away cleanly from the bowl and feels firm but not hard. Cover and set aside in a warm place for 1–2 hours. (The dough will not change much in size or texture, but resting it reduces the elasticity of its gluten.)

3 Place the dough on a floured work surface and divide into 6 equal pieces and roll into balls.

4 Flatten a ball of dough with your hands, then use a rolling pin to roll it into a rough circle about 2mm ($\frac{1}{16}$in) thick.

5 Heat a frying pan or griddle pan over a medium–high heat.

6 Dust any excess flour off the chapatti and place it in the hot pan for about 30 seconds until speckled brown. Keep an eye on the pan – if the pan is too hot, the chapatti will brown instantly. Flip the chapatti over, brush with ghee or oil, if using, and flip again after another 30 seconds. It should be cooked through but not have any burn marks.

7 When done, fold the chapatti in half and place in a lidded container lined with a clean tea towel or kitchen paper. The cloth will absorb the steam and prevent the chapatti from softening. Wipe the pan with kitchen paper and repeat with the remaining chapattis.

Makes 6

Wholemeal flour 250g (9oz), plus extra for dusting
Salt ½ teaspoon
Groundnut oil 1 tablespoon, warmed
Tepid water 150–200ml (5–7fl oz)
Melted ghee or groundnut oil, for spreading (optional)

Note
You can buy good-quality ready-made ones at your local supermarket if you don't have time to make your own.

Types of Lentils

1   Brown lentils
2   Black-eyed beans (lobia)
3   Split moong daal
4   Yellow lentils (toor daal)
5   Whole black urad beans
6   Yellow split peas (channa daal)
7   Pink lentils (masoor daal)
8   White lentils (urad daal)
9   Pigeon pea lentils (loose toor daal)
10 Dried marrowfat peas
11 Puy lentils

UK/US Glossary

aubergine / eggplant

baking parchment / parchment paper

baking tray / baking sheet

beetroot / beet

bicarbonate of soda / baking soda

black-eye beans / black eyed peas

broad beans / fava beans

butter beans / lima beans

butternut squash / butternut pumpkin

cake tin / cake pan

caster sugar / superfine sugar

casserole dish / Dutch oven

chickpeas / garbanzo beans

chilli/chillies / chili/chiles

chilli flake / red pepper flakes

clingfilm / plastic wrap

coriander / cilantro

cornflour / cornstarch

courgettes / zucchini

desiccated coconut / shredded coconut

double cream / heavy cream

electric whisk / electric mixer

filo pastry / phyllo pastry

flour: plain, strong, wholemeal / all-purpose, bread, whole wheat

frying pan / skillet

greaseproof paper / wax paper

griddle pan / grill pan

grill/grilling / broiler/broiling

hob / stove

kitchen foil / aluminum foil

kitchen paper / paper towels

mangetout / snow peas

light muscovado sugar / light brown sugar

natural yogurt / plain yogurt

pepper / bell pepper

rocket / arugula

salad leaves / salad greens

single cream / pouring cream

(oven) shelf / (oven) rack

sieve / strainer

spring onion / scallion/green onion

starter / appetizer

stone / pit

sultanas / golden raisins

swede / rutabaga

tin / pan

Index

Acknowledgements

The bulk of my support has come from Nitin, who stood firm and tall, even throughout his own illness. If it was not for him, I would really struggle to get everything finished. When I began work on the book, I would simply call him up and ask for him to make a note of an idea and to set aside time for me to develop it. That is how so many of my recipes are born. He then typed up my scribbles and scrawls so that I could go back through, retest, adjust and fill in the rest.

Pervin, as usual, is patient and supportive, especially through the long nights and very early rises. During this book, we went on holiday and I was up at 4am sneaking away quietly to work on my recipes and not getting the rest that I perhaps need. But without doing this, the book would have never been complete.

These are the two people that were vital to the book – one is my best friend and the other is one of the most patient humans you could possibly have working with you.